D1360953

My Heart Has Wings

52 Empowering Reflections on Living, Learning, and Loving

Kris King

BridgewayBooks

My Heart Has Wings: 52 Empowering Reflections on Living, Learning, and Loving
Published by Bridgeway Books
P.O. Box 80107
Austin, Texas 78758

For more information about our books, please write to us, call 512.478.2028, or visit our website at www.bridgewaybooks.net.

Library of Congress Control Number: 2008935575

ISBN-13: 978-1-934454-31-2
ISBN-10: 1-934454-31-1

10 9 8 7 6 5 4 3 2 1

I dedicate this, my first book,
to my mom, Rae Case Anderson,
April 10, 1914–May 11, 2007,
and my dad, Arnold Thomas Anderson,
January 21, 1916–October 10, 2001.
You gave me life,
and you gave the best of yourselves to me.
I am blessed beyond measure.
With love and gratitude forever.

—Kris

Table of Contents

An Invitation…

For the past twenty years, I have been developing, designing, and teaching in the field of transformational education and loving every minute of it, even the tough times, because I am constantly learning.

I trust myself as a teacher and learner in the seminar room and have assisted literally thousands of people to make breakthroughs to new levels of consciousness and to take effective action in their lives. I have seen so many miracles! It has been beyond gratifying and an honor to be a part of each person's process.

Integrity is one of my three deepest values, so I believe in practicing what I teach. I have taken many risks in every arena of my life—relationships, physical health, business, finances, travel, photography, the list goes on and on—except one: writing. The idea of writing a book was daunting. I had a long list of reasons that made it impossible for me to write: no one in my family has written a book, who am I to write a book? I won't do it right, it will be terrible, I will be laughed at, it takes too much time, etc. With these thoughts, you can see why I wasn't sitting at my computer at 5:00 a.m.

every day! I had started many times and had much written, and yet I had never completed it. I made it so darn *hard*! I wanted a breakthrough so badly, and yet nothing worked.

All the while, however, I was writing my newsletter articles, writing poems, recording my travels, and taking photos with great ease, delight, and success.

One day, my dear friend Sherrie Frank said, "Why don't we make a book of what you have already written, first?" I was truly dumbstruck. You see, I never thought the process could be easy or fun or shared. I had it in my mind that it was all about me and it was going to be really hard…so it was. Sherrie assisted me to open my mind with one question!

So here it is, a compilation of twenty years of newsletter articles, photos, quotes, and poems that I hope inspire you to open your mind to the importance and possibilities of your life. If there is one thing that touches your heart and mind the way Sherrie's question touched mine, it's all been worth it.

Guess what? My second book, *Little Book for a Big Life*, is next!

With love and gratitude,

Kris King

Ways to Use This Book

I believe we all have different styles of learning, and I believe in teaching in a way that supports many styles at once. I have arranged this book so that you can use it in five different ways, trusting you will read it in the way that works best for you.

First: I placed these fifty-two articles as much as possible in the order that I wrote them. Part of that was for me, to acknowledge the happenings in my life, and part of that was for you. If you choose to read in sequence, you will come to know a bit about how I developed as a person over the years.

Second: You can also focus on one article a week, using the article as a catalyst for exploring your life through your own reflections and writing.

Third: This book is also designed so you can open it up to any page and see what you find for yourself in the moment. Synchronicity.

Fourth: The photos in this book are mostly mine, taken on my trips, in my garden, and of my family and participants. They are paired with quotes that open the door to each article. They say a picture is worth a thousand words. I hope this combination engages your senses, as they have mine.

Fifth: The Reflections portion at the end of each article is for you to learn about yourself, your life, and what you want for yourself now.

I strongly encourage you to do the writing. I have found getting things out of my head and on paper to be very powerful. Such a simple process not only validates the meaning of my own life and yours, but also offers a deeper sense of clarity, which will lead to new behaviors and results.

Give yourself a time-out—no distractions. Sit down, have a cup of tea, relax, and slowly ask yourself each question. Wait a moment before starting your writing; let the answers come. This is just for you, private, so say anything that is true for you in each moment.

Your writing will open your heart and mind to your own life and what you deeply desire. It may lead to heartfelt conversations with the people you love the most. I hope so.

You will notice that I use ellipses often in my writing. There is nothing left out. I use those three periods to represent taking a pause.

I would love to know the impact this book has on you. Your feedback will help me grow as a writer and a contributor to the healing of hearts, minds, and souls. You can e-mail me at kris@wings-seminars.com.

Here we go!

Me during chemotherapy for breast cancer, 1979

Facing Breast Cancer

The breeze at dawn has secrets to tell you.

Don't go back to sleep.

You must ask for what you really want.

Don't go back to sleep.

People are going back and forth across the doorsill

where the two worlds touch.

The door is round and open.

Don't go back to sleep.

—Rumi, translated by Barks

1

⁓⁓

Facing Breast Cancer

December 1992

Sitting here this morning as I write, I wonder why anyone would want to read my story…what audacity to think I could ease your fear or worry by sharing events of my life. I am scared that I won't say things in a way that you will understand or be touched by. I want to remember every detail so I can help you not have the same pain, fear, and loneliness that permeated my whole existence. I don't want you to suffer…there is too much suffering in the world, and I know I cannot take away your pain. I can love you, guide and inspire you, but only you have the power to heal your pain, to change what you feel, think, and want.

What's more, I now realize how my pain helped me change what I was doing. My pain and fear of losing my life helped me transform my life. I don't want to take your pain away. I want you to use it! Learn from it! Use it as a tool of healing instead of a way to hurt yourself more.

I wrote the following in June 1979 while I was in the hospital recovering from my first mastectomy. Visiting hours had just ended with tearful good-byes and lingering looks, a painful mixture of fear and love.

Then it was time for them to go, and I was alone in my room again. The thoughts running through my mind were so numerous, I felt like I was on a roller coaster, the world going by in a blur of ups and downs. Instantly, my mind was transported back in time. I was about ten, and I was with my fourteen-year-old brother Roger and my five-year-old sister Carolyn at Coney Island. We were at the entrance to the biggest roller coaster in the world, the Cyclone, and I was terrified, shaking. I had heard so many awful stories from Roger about all the cars plunging off in a roar of twisted metal and bones, of people falling out to their deaths. I could not imagine why anyone would want to do something that could kill them. Roger kept urging me to do it. He loved to ride in the last car and stand up. Didn't he know he could get hurt and not be my brother anymore? In my heart I screamed, "Don't do it, please don't do it!" but I didn't dare say it out loud because I knew he would laugh at me, and I loved him way too much to have him laugh at me. Instead, I said, "I'm not going and neither is Carolyn, and that's it." I stood just as straight as a soldier, holding my sister's hand so tightly that I knew she couldn't run and join him. I had to protect her! He laughed, and his eyes sparkled with excitement, like he'd won somehow.

And then he was gone, through the turnstile and into the last car where he would have the wildest ride. Heads turned up, our hands squeezed together, we silently watched as the ride began slowly at first and then so quickly disappeared. All we could do was hear the sounds of the wheels on the rails. I was so frightened for him and for me. I loved him so much, I didn't want to lose him. It seemed like an eternity—just that sound, closer then farther away, the riders' screams and moans. I was holding my breath, praying. The sound was getting closer and closer, and then there he was, jumping out of the car onto the sidewalk, safe. He was electric, so full of excitement and laughter. And I could breathe again. Then we were off to the next ride. But I never forgot how frightened I was of losing him.

As quickly as it had come, the vision disappeared. Now I was afraid of losing me. I was holding on tightly and saying, "No, I won't go!" Remembering Roger and Carolyn, our closeness as kids, images of home touched my heart and mind, and I drifted off into a drug-induced sleep.

I was used to waking up in the hospital now, and wondered if that was a good sign or a bad one! Somehow my awareness of time was distorted here. I would fall asleep in the middle of the day after my pain medication, and then I would be half-awake in the night listening to the sounds of the hospital. I could almost hear my body healing. Stitches mending, fluids changing from cloudy with blood to clear, my strength building as the anesthetic gradually was eliminated from my system, and all of this happening without any conscious command from me.

It has now been twenty-nine years since that vision, and I am alive and vibrantly healthy. I did a year of chemotherapy and then a year later had a second prophylactic mastectomy, knowing being alive was more important to me than having breasts. Being my kids' mother was more important to me than my fear of looking different. The possibility of healing my relationship with my husband, Kyle, and my broken heart was stronger than my desire to just disappear.

I decided to live.

1. Can you remember making pivotal decisions in your life? Decisions that led your life in a new direction? What were they?

2. Who do you love so much that you will do whatever it takes to be there for them?

3. What is the impact of your commitment to them on your life?

4. How would you take better care of yourself if your commitment to yourself was as strong as your commitment to them?

Taking the next steps into the unknown, Bhutan

When I Changed My Mind, I Changed My World

If you want your future
to be a repeat of your past,
keep telling your story.
If you want your future
to be a bold and daring
adventure,
start dreaming.
The choice is yours!

— Kris King

2

When I Changed My Mind, I Changed My World

April 1986

There is a space between deciding and doing. I call that space the sea of ambiguity. It can be a challenging space where our decisions meet our deepest fears. How clear and committed we are to creating the result we want will determine how long we swim in this tumultuous sea.

Yes, I fervently decided to live, and no, I didn't know how. So I did the best I could, I set off into the unknown. When my physician told me my breast cancer had metastasized and recommended a year of chemotherapy, I agreed. I also decided to go through it as healthfully as possible. I educated myself on chemotherapy and designed my own vitamin supplement regime with the help of my mother.

Chemotherapy was another roller-coaster ride: two weeks on, two weeks off. Two weeks to feel deathly ill, and two weeks to feel almost human. I worked so hard to seem normal for my husband and boys, cooking meals, making lunches, cleaning house, acting, acting, acting. Then there were the times when I just couldn't keep up the front any longer. In the middle of dinner, playing backgammon, or some small task, I would start to weep, tears rolling down my cheeks and a pain in my heart so intense I thought I would die. And I did think I was dying. When I looked up and saw the horrified looks on my boys' faces, I felt ashamed and so guilty for scaring them. When they would ask me what was wrong, I answered as honestly as I could…"I really don't know." Afraid to tell them I was afraid.

The year went by in a haze of nausea. I was seasick in the sea of ambiguity! I was so committed to coming out of it alive, and I did. For my last night of taking my chemotherapy pills, Cytoxan, I planned a celebration dinner. I was so excited to be done with chemotherapy. I was so eager to get back to feeling like myself again. The night came, and we all had a lovely dinner together, all of us laughing and so happy to have this chapter closed. Then the boys went downstairs to do their homework, Kyle went out to wash the dishes, and I went into the bathroom to take my last two pills. I put them in my hand and really looked at them, the poison that was saving my life. As I looked at them, a terrible realization made its way to the surface…I was on my own now. Really on my own. I swallowed them quickly and went outside, ran as far from the house as possible, and screamed and screamed and screamed.

I was advised that the tissue in my left breast was suspect, and I decided to have a subcutaneous mastectomy and then reconstructive surgery. I remembered the radiation scars on my Aunt Ruby's chest that I saw six months before she died of breast cancer. I knew I wanted to be here, and I wasn't taking any chances. My second surgery was actually easier than my first. Breast cancer was not a shock any longer; it was a reality I wanted to face with all the courage I could muster.

I did the things I knew how to do after my surgery. My goal was to get as physically fit as possible. I changed my diet and started running again, preparing for a half marathon. My body responded so well; I felt my strength growing each day.

But I was still in the sea of ambiguity, swimming toward my goal of health and longevity. During the day my fear was kept at bay only when I was working on something…anything to keep busy. At night, I was completely alone with my fearful and maudlin thoughts. I imagined the very worst: my death, the boys without their mom, Kyle not knowing how to be a good dad, the heartbreak of my parents. Sleep was almost impossible, draining. I woke up in the morning exhausted. My mind was relentless with fear-based disaster films.

One day I had a conversation with dear friends, Sue and Hugh Prichard, that opened a whole new world to me. They told me about a seminar they had just taken. Because I respected them both so much and saw how well they were living their lives together, I thought, I want some of what they have. In just a short period of time, I went to the Personal Effectiveness Seminar with my husband, and what I learned and experienced helped me change my mind about me and my place in the world.

What a revelation it was when I learned that I was living my life with victim thinking. I blamed everything on my husband, my past, and my breast cancer. I had a story, a long one, which cast me in the light of "being done-to" by stronger forces. Poor me. In the four days of the Personal Effectiveness Seminar, I learned how to take ownership of my life, forgive myself and others, make healthy choices, and start dreaming of what I wanted to create for myself instead of for everyone else. It was a profound experience. I came out feeling more energized and alive than I had in years, and I knew this work was for me. I discovered what I wanted to do with my life and the contribution I wanted to make.

When I changed my mind about myself, all of a sudden my whole world changed too. I loved unconditionally instead of with an agenda, and my relationships improved dramatically. I told the whole truth instead of just the part that would get me what I wanted. I started saying yes when I meant it and no when I wanted to. Everything changed for the better, all by changing my mind about myself.

I asked for a job and was told I had some things to work out before I could work there. When the time was right, I was hired, and in two years I owned the company with James. I guess you could say I caught fire and a whole new life began to unfold, a life of accountability and freedom.

Reflections

1. Describe how you react when you decide to do something important and are uncertain or fearful about what to do or how to do it.

2. Starting from the earliest time you can remember, write a list of the most significant events in your life in chronological order.

3. Look at your list and remember the impact of each event, noticing your emotional response to each event.

4. Write a list of the decisions you made about yourself, life, and the world as a result of each event. For example, the world is a safe place or a dangerous place, there's not enough for me or there's plenty for me.

Matthew Spencer King
July 7, 1965–July 14, 1986

Life Will Never Be the Same

I thank my God every time I remember you.
—Philippians 1:3

3

Life Will Never Be the Same

October 1986

In the moment that I saw my son Mark's face on July 14, 1986, I knew my life would never be the same. The sadness and pain I saw there told me a story so heartrending my whole body went silent. Then I heard Mark's words: "Mom, Matt's dead."

The silence shattered. I was surrounded with the sound of my own scream, not truly understanding where the sound was coming from…the cry of a broken heart and of broken dreams.

In that moment of indefinable pain and shock, a moment of such magnitude and desire to deny, my mind began saying, "It can't be true," over and over and over—a mantra of disbelief. How far could I get away from this terrible truth? It was as if I was outside my body watching, not breathing, disconnected.

Then, looking in Mark's eyes, I realized how much my family needed me, needed me to know answers I didn't have. And instantly I came back to the present and the pain.

We faced the tragic reality of Matthew's death from an accidental overdose of his seizure medication, Phenobarbital, not knowing what we were supposed to do. So we just did what we could, drawing together, sharing our sadness and grief, humbly accepting the outpouring of love and compassion that surrounded us.

The details of planning his service helped me stay present. I decided I wanted us to celebrate his life in all its glory and pain, remembering every detail, savoring every shared experience, even the most difficult. I was possessed writing his eulogy. My husband, Kyle, was concerned about me because I didn't want to eat or sleep. I wanted to honor the story of his life the best way I could.

People came. Friends and family arrived from all over the country to be with us in our time of loss, sharing their love simply and profoundly. As the days went by and the reality of Matt's death seeped into my resistant mind, my heart took over.

I felt a place of calm so sweet and tender, so clear and present. My heart knows how much Matthew is loved and that he knows it too. My heart knows how many have shared our loss, their own losses perhaps coming into perspective. In my place of calm, I knew my family was wrapped in a gossamer blanket of love, support, respect, and deep tenderness. The larger family emerged, saddened by the loss of our son and yet joyful that we can draw together and honor life.

Matthew's death has been an awakening beyond all imagining, an opening to the majesty of love and the preciousness of life.

What I wrote for my son's Celebration of Life service:

Matthew Spencer King

July 7, 1965–July 14, 1986

Please be patient with me, my beloved Matthew.

You have moved to a place of infinite patience, grace, and peace, while I and all of us gathered here are deeply feeling the sadness of our loss of you, dear one. Be patient with me, please, because I know I will be in these feelings while I am talking with you now, as I have so many times before.

Remember, we began talking before you were even born. I sang to you with my arms wrapped around me so I could hold you while we danced and moved together. I even introduced you to Beethoven's Symphony no. 3, the *Eroica*, your body moving inside of me, responding to the heroic and passionate sounds. How you surprised me, when after entering this life and I played the same music, I noticed you in you crib, your beautiful little body making the same movement, only more vigorously and elaborately (something you did very well, given more space, you moved right into it and expanded…always testing and experimenting)! I only knew that I loved the music in all its movement and grace. It was only yesterday as I sat looking at the ever-changing sky and thinking of you, I went to play it again and read Beethoven's own simple description of his work. "The *Eroica* Symphony is to celebrate the memory of a great man." We will play the *Eroica* for you, dearest Matthew, today…turning another page, bringing you full circle.

How you loved music! All kinds, from Beethoven and Rachmaninoff to Van Halen and everyone in between, from the very subtle to, in my point of view, the very crude. How you would laugh when I would say, "Matt, I can't stand it anymore! Please, turn it off!" your handsome face cracking into your dazzling smile, mischievous eyes laughing, your elegant body racing down the stairway to turn it down.

I loved to watch you move, dearest Matthew. You moved with such grace, even when you did the jerkiest things. It's like you had this elegant choreographer inside of you, arranging movements that spoke so simply and clearly of you: your beautiful hands telling stories, the night we danced together in Miami, playing and being outrageous together, the muscle dance you did for the Wright brothers from northern California that was so exquisite it brought tears to my eyes. I never knew how beautiful bodies could be until you taught me.

Matthew, you are such a multifaceted being, mercurial, changing in an instant from the deepest and most profound sadness to incredible joy and delight and moving others with you. I remember in my hands and body all the different sensations of holding you and touching you as you grew so rapidly…

Your gurgling laugh when my milk ran from your mouth while you were nursing. You were such a greedy little guy, so eager for learning and new experiences, so willing to go places I was afraid to go. Since you were my firstborn, I feared so much for your safety from the very beginning. I looked in at you in your crib every few minutes to see if you were still there and still breathing, and you always were! Oh, Matthew, you were so full of surprises! Your strong little fingers around mine as you learned to walk and then to run and skip and laugh in the breeze! I realize now that I was a pretty fierce protector.

My dear Matthew, you have been such a teacher for me from the very beginning, such a wise innocent, teaching me so many things I needed to learn. Of all the touches and body sensations that are stored within me, what is strongest right now is the feeling of your arms around me, holding me before you left to go to Houston…holding me safely and gently next to your heart, giving, receiving, and sharing our deep and powerful love for each other. My hands are alive with the vitality and fullness of the beautiful home you created for yourself…your body.

I remember watching you go to the plane, starting another new adventure, not knowing it would be the last time. Little Kyle and I drinking in our last moments with you, our pride in you immense as you set out again to begin, stepping into your manhood with humor, delight, and some fear too, trusting that you knew your way along your path, as we all do. I guess I am rambling a bit, my dear Matthew…and isn't that the way we do it? Exploring different thoughts and feelings together and making a tapestry of our conversations, an ongoing story of what we share together and apart.

In honor and celebration of you today, I want to share with you some of the things that you have taught me in your rich and tumultuous life, for you have been my greatest teacher, the wisest, clearest, most joyful, and profound. I am not saying I always understood…but I have time for that; we all have time for that.

Your family surrounds you now, overfilling this room. As I look now into their eyes, I see only shining love for you, my dearest Matthew, shining love, compassion, and tenderness and also great sadness. All the people you touched were deeply enriched, and if I can put into words one of the greatest lessons and gifts you shared with me and with them, it is that this thing we call life is an ongoing and ever-changing, expanding puzzle so rich and varied that we aren't even sure where all the pieces are. Remember when you used to do paper puzzles? There were times you were voracious and eager to find the solution, angry if it didn't go together immediately and precisely, and other times when you would simply sit back and gaze gently at the pieces, even walk away from it for a while and then come back and solve it so simply. So we put the pieces together in ways we know that seem to fit, sometimes not too well, sometimes brilliantly. Matthew, you taught me to look at different ways to put the pieces together. You were always challenging boundaries. You walked fearlessly where I wouldn't go. It takes great courage to challenge beliefs, and you are truly courageous. (Also a bit pigheaded at times, my dear. Boy, did your dad and I get exasperated with you!)

You have been a constant thread in my life, in our lives, since you joined this family you are loved by. Another gift you taught me about is unconditional love. Love that springs from a place so deep and so clear, there is no end, only more…cool and refreshing as an untouched river, warm and yielding as the tears I have seen slip down your cheeks. Love that nourishes the wildest hunger and soothes ruffled feathers. I believe you came to teach me these things, and you have. When there are no boundaries to love, all is possible. You have taught me to step into places I fear, knowing I am surrounded by all-encompassing, all-surpassing love, as you are today, my beloved son, teacher, friend, guide, and student.

This moment, Matthew—you taught me about this moment, being all there is and ever will be, that I am this moment. Everything I have learned in my life is here in this moment. Matthew, you taught me to celebrate this moment, no matter how things are, to celebrate the love and gifts that surround us, letting them move in and out, flowing about us gracefully. Something else about this moment, Matthew, was your irreverence! Questioning and poking fun at so many of my "supposed to be's." "How come?" was one of your all-time favorites! You packed a lot into your moments: people, visions, experiences, toys, games, humor, love, passion, anger, peace, silence, music, food (I never saw anyone eat so many bananas!). You have helped me learn to fill my moments with the things I value most highly, cherishing each aspect of my life, especially all my relationships and my chosen work.

As I look into the eyes of all your friends today, I know that each one has their own feelings about you and the way you lived among us…and that is as it should be. I believe we are multifaceted beings created by a gentle and loving God, each with our own light within, reflecting a part of the whole. So everyone here has seen parts of you I have never seen, and bringing us together creates a clearer reflection of you, my darling son. You are loved so completely and so dearly. I feel honored and touched that all of us who helped you into this world are with you today to help you move on to another new adventure.

I want to share a poem by E.E. Cummings to tell you, dearest one, how I will travel with you through time.

> i carry your heart with me (i carry it in
> my heart) i am never without it (anywhere
> i go you go, my dear; and whatever is done
> by only me is your doing, my darling)

i fear
no fate (for you are my fate, my sweet) i want
no world (for beautiful you are my world, my true)
and it's you are whatever a moon has always meant
and whatever a sun will always sing is you

here is the deepest secret nobody knows
(here is the root of the root and the bud of the bud
and the sky of the sky of a tree called life; which grows
higher than soul can hope or mind can hide)
and this is the wonder that's keeping the stars apart

i carry your heart (i carry it in my heart)

—E. E. Cummings

Thank you, dearest Matthew, for sharing your time with me.

Reflections

1. What are the awakening events in your life (events that led to great insight and changes in your behavior)?

2. What insights about yourself and life did you have as a result?

3. What changes in your behavior did these realizations lead to, and what has been the positive impact on your life?

Furisode kimono (translates as "swinging sleeves"), the most formal kimono for unmarried women

The Falling Kimono

*For each one of us
there is a star to discover
and a being within ourselves
to bring to life.*

—Janeen Koconis

4

The Falling Kimono

November 1986

The first time the kimono fell, I was surprised. And then I stopped for a moment and remembered fondly how it came to be mine.

In late May 1976, my sister and I went to Hong Kong. It was our first time to take a long journey together and a time to acknowledge a profound transition in her life: her marriage to her childhood sweetheart.

So many aspects of this journey were firsts! Landing in Hong Kong was terrifying—the runway was edged by high-rise apartments! Stepping out into the streets for the first time, my sister and I were two tall Norwegian blondes in a sea of exotic Chinese women and men. This was my first experience of culture shock, of being the one so obviously different than everyone else with no place to hide, and they were all speaking Chinese! The commingling scents in the tropical air were intoxicating, the panorama of the harbor surrounded by mountains was breathtaking, and even the street vendors selling a huge variety of unknown foods were exotic!

Our days unfolded like the petals of a beautiful blossom, laughing, talking, and eating glorious food (she was much better at chopsticks than I and could pick out the best morsels faster than I could blink an eye!). We explored the city by foot, on the Star Ferry, and, of course, did a bit of shopping.

When we entered the silk shop, I had no idea that something significant was happening, that a simple purchase would affect my life so deeply. I was mesmerized by the colors, textures, and exquisite array of items made of silk. After taking time to thoroughly explore the possibilities available to us, Carolyn and I each settled on our purchases. She chose a beautiful embroidered silk organza tablecloth, which she envisioned as her wedding dress. I chose a charming pink kimono with spring flowers that I knew would make a perfect bathrobe.

The second time the kimono fell, I was perplexed, wondering, how did that happen? Then I again stopped for a moment and remembered all the times over the years I had worn it, before it became so tattered that I washed it one last time and put it up on the shelf where I could still see the graceful patterns of spring flowers. I wore it while I held my sons in my arms before they fell asleep, while I cooked breakfast for them before they went off to school, while I comforted them from something that was hurtful or scary, and while I watched them open packages on Christmas morning with faces filled with delight. So many moments…moments filled with love, tenderness, and deep connection with my family. These moments are the reason I kept it even though it was worn through in many places. The kimono was filled with our shared love.

The third time the kimono fell, I was stunned. I looked over my shoulder, wondering what was going on. Then I became aware that my kimono had been sitting quietly on that shelf for years, never falling as I opened my closet. And here in four days time—the four days since Matthew's death—it had fallen three times. My grief overwhelmed me. I picked up my worn kimono, soft as water, held it to my heart just the way I so deeply wanted to hold Matthew and never would again.

An intake of breath, my skin tingled, my heart clamored, and I knew I was experiencing my deep spiritual connection to Matthew…and his presence. Call it a dream, call it reality; it was a turning point for me and my understanding of death. In that moment I also knew that my Matthew would be wrapped for eternity in our shared memories of love.

I would make a silken bag to hold my son's ashes, and it would be created from the kimono I was holding so closely to my heart. The only thing new would be multicolored ribbons, one for each of his twenty-one years. This silken bag with ribbons would hold the history of my son's life tenderly through time.

A sense of calm filled me.

Reflections

1. Remember a time when your intuition told you something significant was happening, where all of a sudden you felt a deep emotional connection and knew it was time to pay attention in a different way. Describe this event.

2. What was the impact of this event in your life?

3. Who do you love enough to go the extra mile for, to do your very best to care for them? What is the impact in that relationship?

Goddess in the garden, Kyoto, Japan

Magical Holidays?

*Each separate being in the universe
returns to the common source.
Returning to the source is serenity.*
                    —Lao Tzu

5

Magical Holidays?

With the holidays fast approaching, have you noticed any changes in your thoughts and feelings? The changes could be really small—like looking for cookie recipes—to really major—like starting to sweat over your financial situation. Do you realize how many thousands of images and experiences you have associated with this celebratory time of year?

We are surrounded by media and cultural expressions of how our holidays are supposed to be: magazines filled with sumptuous pictures of fantastically decorated homes and tables laden with rich and exquisite foods and spirits, shop windows displaying shimmering festive clothing meant to be worn to parties with laughing, attractive friends. Everywhere we look we are encouraged to buy the perfect gift, however durable, precious, or exotic, all the while having our ears filled with the sounds of angels and Rudolf.

What happens when you are enveloped by all of these expressions of how holidays are "supposed to be" celebrated? What happens when the outside images don't line up with your own past experiences and beliefs? If your holidays delight and fulfill you completely, read no further, pick up your

42

pen, and tell me how you do it! Most of us feel some level of frustration, anxiety, loneliness, or maybe even a sense of coming up short (in more ways than financially). These are some of the feelings that occur when your perceptions and experiences don't line up with the "supposed to be's." We experience ourselves outside the common frame of reference; our expectations are not met.

So what can we do? Here are some of the many choices: just do nothing, resign yourself—"It will always be like this"—or "If I plan far enough ahead maybe it won't be so bad," or bootstrap yourself into the common frame of reference—"I'm doing it by the book, the right way, and of course I'm happy. *#@(%!" Or you could create your own frame of reference, one that is a true expression of you: "I'm going to enjoy the holidays in a new way this year."

Sounds great, only how do we do it? Start by asking yourself some questions that will lead you to describing how you want your holidays to be, not how the ads or mom or the department store wants it to be. For instance, "How do I want to feel when I give a gift to Mom?" or "How will my home look when I finish decorating?" or "How will my savings account look come January 1?" Within every question lies an answer that will lead you to the appropriate action. Here's a sample answer to the first question: "I want to feel proud and loving when I give Mom her gift. Mom loves things I've made with my own hands, and I am proud of my woodwork. While I am carving, I will think of how much I love her, and my love will show through my work!" When you ask yourself defining questions and listen to the answers, you will notice your level of frustration diminishing, your level of clarity and ease rising.

Once you have answers that satisfy you, that feel comfortable when you think about them, and that please you when you talk about them, it's time for action. Remember, you have an unlimited range of behaviors and feelings to choose from, the expanse between opposites. The opposite of frustration is enthusiasm, of anxiety is anticipation, of loneliness is involvement, and of coming up short is abundance. Look at all the options linking these opposites together! Lying at midpoint between all these options is neutral ground, a simple place of peace and self-acceptance. This is the place you source from. Every now and then, stop and notice how you feel when you pay attention to your own answers and act on them. Wouldn't it be delightful if creating your own frame of reference was simple and exciting?

My whole life changed when I changed one behavior. I started giving cleanly what I wanted most to receive: love and respect. You are your own most exquisite and precious gift. By sharing yourself with others, your gifts are released and all are enriched immeasurably.

Since you are always doing something anyway, why not do the things you really want to do? Be as gentle and supportive with yourself as you are with others; begin to create your own celebration. Joy, like any other feeling, is an inside option and a choice—so is magic!

Reflections

1. What were your experiences of holidays when you were a kid? What was wonderful about them and what was difficult?

2. What messages did you receive from family, friends, school, and perhaps religion that are still true for you? Are there any messages that you resisted, wanting to create your own meaning of holidays?

3. How do you feel when you pay attention to your own answers to the question, "What do I want?" and act on them?

4. What is one thing you will do today to experience more joy? You deserve it!

Kalachakra mandala, Bhutan

The Party's Over.
Now What?

The more simple we are,
the more complete we become.
—Auguste Rodin

6

The Party's Over.
Now What?

February 1987

Christmas and Hanukkah are over, the decorations are put away (unless you are one of those wonderful people who stay lit up all year!). The incredible-amazing-best-ever-year-end-sales are done too…and how are you? The tender you, the you who may pull the covers over your head in a thunderstorm, the you who may pretend not to see your best friend on a blue day, or the you who may "know" all the things you "should" do for yourself and yet don't. What happens when the "party" is over and you go home?

Part of me is just now mending from the holidays, our first holiday without our son Matthew. Being with my husband, our boys, Mark and Kyle, my mom and dad, sister and brother and their children was a gift. Each one is so unique, beautiful, talented, and bright. In the midst of all their love and merriment, I heard my tender part whisper to me about Matthew. In some moments, his lack of presence was somehow more apparent to me than the presence of my laughing and cherubic nieces. I would catch myself and bring myself back to share in the giggles and dancing with tears drying on my cheeks.

Then I realized my loss is as real as their presence and it is all right to feel both. I am honoring all of me rather than denying the whispers of loneliness.

So the "party" ended and I came home, savoring the silence and missing the noise. I talked to myself a lot, feeling as if part of me was missing…and it is. At times loving seems a lot easier than letting go.

I decided to focus on the love part. We don't need specific dates to make it okay to love someone, do we? So I filled our home with friends, strangers (who became friends), good food, and a lot of laughter (created by the help of a great game, Pictionary, and very outrageous players). As I found myself giving to those I welcomed into our home, my tender part started to heal.

One of the things Matthew's death taught me is to honor life, all of it in each moment. As I do this consciously, my life is enriched immeasurably. I don't need to wait until Valentine's Day to tell you how much I love you and hold you dearly in my heart, and I don't need to wait until Chinese New Year to eat fortune cookies! This life is meant for living and living in your own way. You are the one who defines what "party" means.

Each of us honors life in our own way. Does your way reflect who you really are?

I bless the earth and all her people
holding all with tenderness and grace,
with respect for all of life
and spirit

I am blessed in my marriage
two souls joining and independent
two hearts compassionate and true
two spirits soaring!

I bless the sun and the moon for
lighting my life
creating warmth
And the crystal night for
making space for my dreams.
　　　　　　　　　—Kris King

Reflections

1. Have you ever wanted to "pull the covers over your head" and not get up? Hoping "it" would all just go away? What were the "its"?

2. If you could have one thing in your life be different than it is, what would you pick? Why?

3. Each of us honors life in our own way. Does your way reflect who you really are? What do you do to express your appreciation for life?

Cactus, *Opuntia monacantha*, Bhutan

Great ideas, it has been said,
come into the world as gently as doves.
Perhaps then, if we listen attentively,
we can hear, amid the uproar
of empires and nations,
a faint flutter of wings,
the gentle stirring of life and hope.
—*Albert Camus*

7

Desert Bloom

March 1987

With the wind in my face and the sun still at my back, I have returned from the desert. It was an experience that is not yet over. As a matter of fact, it is still beginning.

I gave myself a wilderness time-out as a celebration of my Personal Effectiveness Seminar graduation five years ago, the beginning of my journey into self-trust, self-awareness, and celebrating life.

This is what it was like for me, a tenderfoot in the wilderness, to go on such an adventure.

Preparations for a wilderness adventure begin with gathering your equipment together. What a trip that was! I borrowed everything from everyone I knew. I took things that belonged to each member of my family so I could feel their presence whenever I wanted to: a sleeping bag from my son Kyle, long underwear from my son Mark, a long-sleeved shirt from my husband, Kyle, a friend's backpack, and on down the line. When I had it all spread out on the bedroom floor, it looked like it would never fit into the backpack, but it did! Visions of Mount Vesuvius lurked in my mind as I thought about opening it.

Off we go, meeting all the others who had chosen the same adventure, smiling, laughing. Not knowing what to expect, we climbed on board and took flight, descending into balmy Palm Springs several hours later. We were greeted by bougainvillea blossoms, hibiscus, and oleander scenting the evening air and splashing yards with exquisite color. My senses were totally enveloped by the lushness, my mind by curiosity. What are these days with myself all about? How will I be spending my time? Is there something specific I am looking for? What is it? Will I like the me I discover?

The next morning we drove leisurely into Joshua Tree National Monument (later renamed a national park). I emphasize our pace as leisurely because we all had started a process of slowing down, quieting ourselves. There was an unspoken agreement of introspection and wonder at the majesty of the desert unfolding before us. This agreement lasted and deepened during our time with the desert.

I keep asking myself if there are appropriate words to describe my experience. There are, and they will never be able to "fill" you as I was filled by the exhilaration of feeling, doing, touching, hearing, looking, laughing, crying, and being more peaceful than I can remember. Frequently, at home, I have the feeling that my attention is going in seventeen different directions. I gave myself freedom to be alone and to join, and when I did either, I did it completely. The sensation of wholeness in each moment permeated everything.

The desert is a subtle place perfectly balanced with the elements. Everything you see "fits." Before going to the desert, I knew I could appreciate it, but I never thought I could come to love such a "harsh" place. I was mistaken. When I took my first walk alone, I was stunned by the life and the beauty that surrounded me. In April, the desert blooms. There were flowers everywhere, under my feet, under the rocks, hidden in nooks and crannies, splashes of intense indigo and throbbing red. Cacti so wrapped in spines they looked painful were flirting with everyone who came by, their scented blossoms whispering. Whispering speaks of the subtleties, of the wind and how "harsh" became majestic.

A pair of crows nested high in the rocks above our camp, and their movements taught me a profound lesson. I had never heard the sound of the air moving beneath a bird's wings before, so many other sounds envelop me at home. In the desert, as I lay watching these blacker than black birds, I could hear the sounds of their wings moving through the air and I wondered, "What are the sounds of my own being that I do not hear?"

As I lay watching and wondering, ants walked by busy as ever, other crows joined my two crows and performed miraculous aerobatics. Moving my hand beneath my head, I realized that tiny yellow and white blossoms were a carpet beneath my head. My world was whispering to me, gently teaching me.

My wilderness experience is not over yet, as a matter of fact, it beckons me to remember "now."

Reflections

1. What are your clearest memories of being nourished by being in nature? Where were you? Who were you with?

2. How often do you give yourself alone time to reflect? If you don't, what do you do instead?

3. How do you feel when you are alone? Do you like the company you keep?

4. If you could be anywhere in the whole wide natural world right now, where would you be? Why?

Precious lotus, Ko Samui, Thailand

Awakening brings its own assignments,
unique to each of us,
chosen by each of us.
Whatever you may think about yourself, and
however long you may have thought it,
you are not just you.
You are a seed, a silent promise.

> —Marilyn Ferguson,
> The Aquarian Conspiracy

8

What's So Scary about the Truth?

August 1987

Come with me on a journey, a journey to a very special place, a place where the words spoken are words of truth, where the actions are demonstrations of the truth, that everything you see and feel and hear is all the truth, and all the truth is given with love. Give yourself a moment to truly imagine such a place. Sitting here at my typewriter and thinking about such a place touches me deeply; so much so that the front of my shirt is wet with tears and my heart is full. Is that the idealist in me speaking? Is there a yearning in each of us that wants to know we are living with the truth, and the truth is based in love?

For a major portion of my life, I thought that I was the most honest person in the world and, naturally, prided myself on it, because I never told a lie. It was a rude awakening for me when I learned in the Personal Effectiveness Seminar that all those things I thought and never said—because someone might not like it, or they might not like me, or I wouldn't get my own way—were really lies.

I was truly stunned, and I knew it was true. I had withheld my own truth because I didn't think I could stand what would happen. I feared other's judgments, anger, and abandonment. I had learned how to be "nice."

What did I do with my revelation? All those responses from others were still possible, right? On the other hand, I knew how invisible the real me felt when I withheld the truth. Time to choose. Step by step, interaction by interaction, I tried the truth out, keeping two simple thoughts as my guides:

1. The truth given without love is simply judgment.
2. The truth not listened to is self-denial.

Have you ever wondered how to build your self-respect? Well, as I progressed in my journey with the truth, I noticed that I was valuing myself more and more. I was even listening to what I had to say!

What's so scary about the truth? That someone may not like you, that someone might have a different point of view? What I now think is really scary is that I could live this life and not be known for who I really am, that my dreams and visions could go unrealized all because I was afraid of what could happen. That made my choice easy.

On my journey with the truth, I have learned another lesson. Listening to the truth of others with love is just as important as telling the truth with love. When I get defensive, it makes it unsafe for the other person to speak their truth. Does this mean all you hear is the truth? You are the only one who will know.

As I go through my days, reading the newspaper and noticing how we as individuals, employees, citizens, etc., respond in our daily lives, I am having a growing sense of urgency about how we value the truth. The place you saw when we went on our imagined journey is a possibility only if each of us creates it within ourselves.

It sounds so simple and it is; that doesn't mean it's easy.

Reflections

1. What is it about telling the whole, microscopic truth that stops you from telling it? What could happen?

2. In which parts of your life is it easy to tell the whole truth? And what is the impact of telling the whole truth?

3. In which parts of your life is it most difficult to tell the whole truth? And what is the impact when you don't?

4. Who are your best role models for telling the truth? What is it you most admire about them?

My son, Matthew, at three-and-a-half

How Long Does It Take to Heal?

Merry Mattie
  in a sack,
  his eyes light up,
  his arms go back.
Pixy laughter, sheer delight.
Adorable cherub…
  good night, good night.
            —Ruby Groom,
            Matt's great-aunt

9

How Long Does It Take to Heal?

September 1987

Today is the first day of September, not very fall-like at all—the temperature is soaring. School starts next week, notebooks and glue are in short supply, and the awareness of changing seasons surrounds us. This is a time of reflection for me…memories of all the other times that school started since I became a mother twenty-two years ago. There is something very poignant about this year for me. It has been a little over a year since my son, Matthew, died, and it has been just a week since I saw my son, Mark, off for his first year of college at Duke University. Somewhere inside of me these two occurrences have collided, overlapping snapshots blurring my vision.

Thinking I was mostly healed after Matt's death, this collision and the new feelings I have stunned me. "How long does it take to heal?" I ask myself over and over. I know Mark is starting on a great adventure and setting a course for his own life, and that delights me. Yet lurking somewhere is this fear, this "no name" fear. I am even afraid to say it. Will saying it make it true? "Will I lose Mark too?"

I find myself staring out windows, gazing into the distance, not really knowing what I am looking for. If I look far enough, what will I see? Perhaps the ending of an intricate and loving pattern of personalities and moments, of good times and bad. Maybe there is something new on the horizon that I want to identify. Whatever it is, it is not clear yet. So I keep on gazing, listening to all the sounds of my being. My heart says, "The healing isn't done yet. Give yourself some more time. Patience."

I know I am in the process of designing a new way of being that fits. Do you ever try to hold on to the illusion that everything is just the same as it was, long after it has changed? This year I have learned that the longer I hold on to the illusion, the longer the healing takes, like reopening a wound over and over. If I try to keep Matthew alive all day in my thoughts, somehow he always dies at night and I go through all the pain again. If I try to keep Mark safe forever, he'll never realize his dreams.

One night as I lay looking at the stars and constellations brilliant overhead, I asked them for help. "Let me love Matthew as deeply as ever and let him go so I can heal." In the morning, I awoke realizing I only see the stars in the darkness. The stars are there always, moving through time with us, surrounding us with their beauty and light and mystery. It takes the darkness to see their light. This majestic transformation I witness daily lets me know I am surrounded by love even when I don't see it. Matt is like the stars.

And I realize now, it is not Matt that I want to release. He is a part of my life forever. It is my pain I choose to release.

How long does it take to heal? Perhaps it is time to let go of the question. Thank you for moving through time with me. Even when I don't see you, I know you are there. Just like the stars.

Reflections

1. Who have you loved and lost, to death or the end of a relationship?

2. How did this ending affect you?

3. How long did it take you to heal? Have you?

4. What have you learned about yourself and life as a result that you can take forward to create fulfilling relationships?

My mom and dad dancing together. Rae and Arnold Anderson, 1995.

Thanks, Mom and Dad

The privilege of a lifetime
is being who you are.
—Joseph Campbell

10

Thanks, Mom and Dad

February 1988

Looking out the window at the beginning of spring, the cycles of the year gently progressing, my childhood pops brightly into my thoughts. I had a great time being a kid, and I had a lousy time being a kid. What I am coming to realize is that the lousy times helped me grow up and become a strong person (back then it just felt hard!).

My mom, Rae, was born in a log cabin in Range, Oregon, a place that no longer exists. Her parents, Mabel and Lou Case, were of pioneer stock; their parents crossed the plains in covered wagons. My dad, Arnold, was born in Tacoma, Washington, to Inga and Olaf Anderson, who both came here as teenagers from Norway. All of them were seeking a better way of living freer, more self-directed and creative. They all faced and lived up to hard times, the moments of laughter and love seeing them through.

My mom went off to Whitman College when she was sixteen and was a Phi Beta Kappa by the time she was nineteen. She was a high school chemistry teacher by the time she was twenty! My dad put himself through Pacific Lutheran and became a teacher of music and geography. Education was a pivotal focus in their lives. They were both teaching in East Stanwood when they met, fell in love, got married, and had to pretend that they were not (back then you couldn't be a married woman and be a teacher).

Then my dad learned to fly! World War II was raging in Europe, and my dad started taking flying lessons in a Piper Cub. He was so good he became a flight instructor. Then he was hired as a pilot for Pan American World Airways, and their world changed dramatically. No more thoughts of living in the Northwest and teaching together as life goals. They too became pioneers, much like their parents and their parents' parents before them.

My world growing up revolved around my dad's schedule. There were certain things we only did when he was home, like taking the boat out for fishing and picnics, or going to New York City to see the Rockettes at Radio City Music Hall. While my dad was gone, my mom did everything for us, and I saw all her strengths and competencies as well as her love.

What's this story about? I guess I am realizing that what mom and dad gave me was something bigger than a safe and comfortable home, love, discipline, and opportunities to learn. By their actions, their way of living each day, they taught me that I could make my life be any way I wanted it to be.

They gave me the two things I needed most to make the choices that brought me to this spring day.

> There are only two lasting bequests
> we can hope to give our children.
> One of these is roots,
> the other, wings.
> —Hodding Carter Jr.

It has taken a while, and many exhilarating, heartbreaking, and sometimes puzzling detours. Thanks to you and all you have given me, my life is immensely rich, rewarding, and filled with adventures, loving people, fulfilling work, and the faith to take risks.

Thank you for being my mom and dad.

Reflections

1. What do you know about your parents' origins and histories? Write it down.

2. What do you admire and respect about each parent? When you focus on these aspects, how do you feel?

3. What judgments do you have of each parent? When you focus on these aspects, how do you feel?

4. When you look back at your time with your parents, what are you grateful for?

Red dragonfly in my garden

A Pebble or a Gem?

Put your heart, mind and soul
into even your smallest acts.
This is the secret of success.
　　　　　　—Swami Sivananda

11

A Pebble or a Gem?

April 1988

Has this ever happened to you?

You are reading along, agreeing with the material, finding it fairly interesting, and then your perspectives about things start to expand, your curiosity is piqued, and you become fully engaged with what you are reading. Then all of a sudden a phrase literally jumps off the page at you! Larger than life and much larger than any bold print, because the sentence is almost like a collision—thoughts, perspectives, feelings, insights, and understanding coming together all at once. The pieces of a puzzle fall into place (you might not have even known you were missing a piece!), and you have a profound sense of clarity, a lightness of being, an expansion of your consciousness. In that moment everything changed.

Aren't we incredible! Seemingly unrelated information and events coming together, creating insight and the potential for simple and profound courses of action that can add great meaning and experience to our lives. These times are truly times to savor and to be thankful for. A child might clap their hands and burst out laughing, or be wondrously silent, gazing off into the unseen distance. An adult may exclaim "Eureka!" and run off to find someone to share the new insight with or grab their journal and write it all down to make sure they remember every single aspect.

Have you ever had this fantastic experience and wanted to instantly share it with someone? So you race to find that special person. They read it, look at you quizzically, and say, "What are you so excited about?" To you, this information is a precious gem, crystalline and pure, penetrating directly to personal clarity. To your friend, it looks like one of millions of pebbles on the beach, interchangeable, nondescript, a mere shoulder shrug! How odd. When that happens, how do you feel? Deflated in some way, perhaps even a loss of enthusiasm.

Remember *Illusions*, a great book about consciousness, by Richard Bach? I agree with Don Shimoda, the enlightened barnstormer, when he says, "You can do it with any book…if you read carefully enough…hold some problem in your mind, then open any book handy and see what it tells you." We are surrounded by helpful information in so many forms: music, literature, science, art, films, mathematics, silence, nature. All we need to be is open to it.

So it is no wonder our answers, our gems, are someone else's pebbles. They are involved with their lives and finding their own gems, solutions to their own puzzles. What I would encourage you to do the next time someone you care about comes to you with their new insight is to look for the gem instead of finding the pebble. Be curious and supportive and watch them light up!

Sometimes there are gems so elegant and precise they touch many deeply.

I would like to share a gem with you that stunned me in its simplicity and power and has become a touchstone in my life.

"Given the situation, the event, the circumstances…how do I be the very best me possible?"

A pebble or a gem, it's up to you.

1. Have you ever had an important realization, wanted to share it, and had some-one not "get it"? What was the realization(s)?

2. How did you feel about yourself in that moment when they didn't "get it," and how did you feel about them?

3. What does it take for you to hold your own excitement even when others do not agree? How do you do it?

Goddess protector at Taktsang Monastery, Bhutan

"I'll tell you what I think," said Wiggin.
"I think you don't grow up until
you stop worrying about
other people's purposes or lack of them
and find the purposes you believe in for yourself."
—Orson Scott Card, Xenocide

12

Time to Reflect

September 1988

I just returned from a few days of vacation up in the San Juan Islands at Friday Harbor, Washington. I went to visit my mom and dad by seaplane from Seattle, which stirred old memories of flying as a child with my dad in his Piper Cub through the Florida Keys! If you ever want to discover the beauty of the San Juans from a different perspective, I highly recommend flying in a seaplane (they supply the earplugs!).

Looking out the window, 75–150 feet above the water, I saw many things in a different light, elevated. Above the trees instead of in them, above the coastline instead of walking it, looking down and seeing the geological patterns of rock and earth, the clusters of homes, the wake of a ferry bringing vacationers to play and explore. Patterns of life revealed.

My whole time away was like that, taking time to look at things from a different perspective. Spending time with my mom and dad without the responsibilities of being wife, mother, teacher, or business owner—just being me—was exquisite. We had time to be together in a way that words cannot express. Yes, my parents are growing older, as am I, and to spend time appreciating each other, both quietly and boisterously, filled a space that had been waiting to be filled for all of us. To share dinner conversation with their friends and to listen to their concerns for our country, our children, and our future opened more new perspectives.

As I listened, watched, and interacted with my folks and their friends, I became aware of a new sensation in my body that I had never felt before with my folks. I was relaxed and peaceful…nothing to prove. My goodness, I felt like an adult, an equal in the presence of my parents! I was giddy with the awareness.

Another realization quickly followed. In my desire to prove my worth to my parents (and anyone else who happened to be around), I had narrowed my focus to things I could intellectually prove were right. Ouch, self-righteousness!

Have you ever gotten so involved in your own way of thinking, feeling, and acting that you forgot there are many other ways of doing things? When I forget to listen and open my eyes, my world narrows instantly. My task, way of doings things, way of feeling, etc., seems like the only way. I defend, justify, and explain, and I distance myself from those I care most about.

When we took my parents' boat out of Mitchell Bay and into the sound to fish and check the crab pots, I held these two discoveries in my mind. I stood at the stern of the boat silently watching everything, breathing in the pure air. Finally, my eyes settled on the wake of the boat. There is an old saying that every moment holds the stuff of enlightenment. The wake reminded me of the wake each of us creates as we move through this world, our impact. Looking at the wake set into motion a whole series of questions I asked myself while I relaxed and spent time looking at clouds.

What kind of a wake do I create?

Do I take the time to notice how my behavior affects those around me?

When I am out in the world, do I value the people who have different points of view?

Do I invite new information and learning?

How wide open is my perspective, my heart, and my attention to the wake I create?

After being with these questions for the remainder of my visit, I made three deep commitments to myself:

1. To use my personal power authentically, maintaining my sense of equality with my parents.
2. To be curious and open-minded, accepting myself instead of proving myself.
3. To give myself the precious time to reflect, for in those moments I find truer ways of being my simple self.

No matter how full our lives are, we all deserve quiet time to reflect, to quietly try on new perspectives and notice if they fit, to expand our worldview and invite learning.

Reflections

1. How often do you give yourself the gift of a true time-out? Nothing to do except be with yourself?

2. What are the questions you would ask yourself if you gave yourself the gift of time to reflect?

3. What are the questions you resist asking yourself? Why?

Prayers for well-being released to the wind, Bhutan

The past is history.
The future is a mystery.
Today is a gift.
That is why we call it the present.
—Eleanor Roosevelt

13

Simple Gifts

September 1988

Do you believe in magic? I do.

Let's pretend we have a magic wand! And when we wave it, all these simple gifts will be ours—every one of them! Things for us to share and treasure for a lifetime or for one exquisite moment.

- The gurgling laughter of a newborn child, radiantly trusting and eager, tiny fingers grasping yours without question
- Discovering that the book you are reading is so wonderful, you never want it to end
- The first whiff of wood smoke heralding the coming of fall
- The wag of a tail, a woof of welcome, a ball dropped at your feet…play with me!
- Finding the perfect gift for a friend, something you know they will cherish
- The poetry of Kahlil Gibran, E. E. Cummings, Emily Dickinson, Hafiz, of life. Rich words that draw you deeper into the mystery
- The vibrant hues of sundown, blazing across an evening sky…the dawn not far away

- A deep sigh of enjoyment and appreciation—a job well done
- The pull of the stars and planets as they gleam boldly in the heavens
- A hand outstretched to you, warm, welcoming, beckoning, just for you
- Heartfelt, belly-shaking laughter, contagious and inviting
- Tilling the soil and preparing it for planting, nurturing, and watching your garden grow
- Standing before the creation of a master in deep appreciation of their commitment and their courage to be seen
- Holding someone close to your heart, without words or expectation, reverent connection
- Beholding the miracle of a teardrop sliding down the cheek of a stranger or one you love
- Frost painting pictures on the windowpane, crystallized moments
- The creation of a wave folding and crashing its way to shore, its thunder filling the salty air
- Laugh lines at the corners of wise eyes—deep, clear, and irreverent
- Robust souls lifting their voices in song, telling part of life's story
- Observing someone do a kindness for another and feeling your heart swell with tenderness
- The first tentative steps of a child, focused, wavering, succeeding
- The wind dancing and soaring, playing with autumns leaves, a whirlwind of color
- Eyes, beautiful eyes, gazing at the mystery that surrounds us, seeing more than the eye can see
- Family, community, sitting together, hands held in gratitude and reverence for the abundance of our lives and relationships
- Sharing a meal prepared with love, a glass of wine, and free-flowing conversation with friends
- Catching the eye of someone you love from across the room and smiling your secret smile
- The moment of recognition that all life is connected and divine and you are part of it all
- Feeling the surge of excitement and exhilaration that comes with taking a risk and succeeding

Simple gifts, simple treasures that cost nothing and yet fill our lives with magic. Are there more? Yes. The list is unending and begins the moment you wake up each morning.

Reflections

1. What things would you add to your list of simple gifts?

2. Are these things you enjoy alone or with others? When is your experience most intense?

3. How do "simple things" enrich your experience of life?

4. When your expectations are not met, what do you do?

Asking for conscious use of the environment, Bhutan

Your life is at stake…
the worst thing you could do
is live out someone else's life
thinking it was your own.

—David Whyte

14

Signposts and Signals

Have you ever wondered how you've gotten where you are? Scratched your head and asked yourself out loud, "How did this come to be?" It could be that something wonderful has just happened, or something not so wonderful, maybe even awful. Confusion, or the "fog," settles in all about your brain and nothing seems to make any sense. Sound familiar? Me too!

It's taken me years to learn some pretty simple lessons. And simple does not mean easy. The awareness is simple; taking action may be challenging.

One lesson is there are signposts and signals all along the way to guide us through life, whether we choose to be aware of them or not.

A signpost is a choice point, an X on the map, a time to decide yes or no to something we are being offered, an avenue to different opportunities, an opening to change. Many of us think of signposts as major events: should I get married, take the new job, move to a different city, have children, write a book? What I am learning is signposts are everywhere, and moment to moment we are surrounded by opportunities to interact with our world. It is the choices we make at simple signposts that direct the course of our lives and determine whether or not we live according to our deepest values.

How do we choose, consciously, unconsciously, or both? When we choose unconsciously, we are stuck in our repetitive patterns of thought, feeling, and behavior. Perhaps thinking, "This is just the way it is, always has been, always will be." The outcome of this is what we call "stuck." When we choose consciously, we pause, evaluate consequences and results, pros and cons, and if what we are evaluating is inside our ethics and values. One of the biggest considerations is whether it is something that fills our heart and soul. Vacillating between the two ways of choosing is confusing and frustrating.

A signal is a message your body gives you to tell you that you are at a signpost! That it is time to wake up and pay attention to what is right in front of you. For example, what messages does your body send you when you are thinking about breaking an agreement with someone you care about, or when you want something you know is not good for you, or you are telling a lie? When you are watching something on the news that completely goes against your principles? Perhaps a tightening of your gut, increased heart rate, perspiration, anxiety, shortness of breath. How does your body let you know you are at a choice point? These are signals your unconscious is sending you to be present now because "this is important."

I used to bump into things all the time, break things, drop things, not get things finished on time, lose things, forget everything, run out of gas, get sick, have headaches…sound familiar? You have your own signal system that is "trying" to assist you to wake up and stay true to yourself, your values, and your greater good. Do you listen? And what happens when you don't?

This is where the simplicity ends. No one can tell you what your signposts and signals are. You are the only one who knows and the only one who can choose the course of your life! And that is the good news!

This is not an appeal for all of us to get head-bound, trying to figure it all out; it is an appeal for us to listen to our signals and to choose at the signposts with respect for ourselves and the people we love. Imagine how different our world would be if each person was choosing with such attention and respect.

A signpost stands before us all. Do we want to live together on a peaceful, healthy planet, where different cultures and ways of living are valued, respected, acknowledged, and even learned from? How will you choose? Will you listen to and take action based on the signals your heart, mind, and spirit are sending you?

If that question is too ethereal for you, bring it closer to home. Will you listen to and take action in your closest relationships based on the signals your heart, mind, and spirit are sending you?

Reflections

1. Identify important signposts in your childhood, young adulthood, and recently.

2. How did you choose at each one—consciously, unconsciously, or a bit of both? Did you create what you wanted?

3. How does you body let you know there is something to pay attention to? Do you listen?

4. What have you learned from your choices and consequences?

5. In what part of your life is it most difficult for you to see the signposts? What is the result?

Ancient chorten, Bhutan

The finest and noblest ground
on which people can live is truth;
the real with the real;
a ground on which nothing is assumed.
— Ralph Waldo Emerson

15

Above the Clouds

March 1989

By the time you read this, I will no longer be "above the clouds." I will be descending from the peak of Mt. Jaljale, 14,700 feet up in the Himalayas, my eyes resting on some of the highest mountain peaks in the world—Everest, Lhotse, and Makalu.

As I write, I am still in a state of preparation for this incredible journey, and surprise of surprises, the preparation is a vast learning experience! The insights I have had while preparing to leave my husband, children, family, work, staff, all of you, and our culture for a whole month have come softly and profoundly, sneaking up "on little cat feet" (as Carl Sandburg described the fog rolling into Chicago).

Three years ago, the opportunity to go trekking in Nepal for thirty days presented itself, and I wanted to go. I evaluated my life and told myself, "I don't have the time, and I don't have the money" (the great American excuses for not having the life you want). I supported those going on the trip and went to the airport to see them off on their journey. As I watched them board the plane, my heart was breaking. I wanted so very much to be on that plane with them! When I saw the tires leave the runway, a little voice in my head said, "I belong on that plane. Next time, I am going!"

Three years passed, and the opportunity presented itself again. I still didn't have the time and the money when I evaluated my life, and yet I wanted to go. My first insight came when I realized how I made the journey become a reality this time, instead of a dream that I have had since I was a child. I said yes to my dream instead of no! I said, "Yes, I am going!" every time I faced an obstacle, a fear, or a doubt. I said it out loud, I said it to other people, and most importantly, I said it to me.

And all of a sudden, amazing things began to happen. So many people supported me to go. They wanted me to have my dream come true. Family, friends, co-workers, participants in seminars, even my dry cleaner!

Everything fell into place. My business partner, James Newton, helped me in many ways: time away from work, finances, and encouragement. My husband, Kyle, knowing how important this trip was to me, told me he would handle home and taking care of our sons. Surprise, a dear friend, Meredith Bliss, who was going on the trip, had thousands of free miles and gave me a ticket. My intention was so clear, I could feel it. Sounds amazingly easy, right? Why, of course! That's plain to see, and yet that's not what I do consistently. Very often I have mixed intentions, part of me wanting to go forward and part of me pulling back. No wonder I was creating mixed results. I saw very clearly how I stop myself from creating what I want and how easy it is to turn around. Clear intention!

I found myself out in the future a great deal, anticipating, eager for new experiences and learning, and getting ready. My second insight came with a sudden shift of focus. As departure time came closer, instead of looking forward, I started looking back. The importance of leaving with my life in order became paramount—touching people, making phone calls, writing notes, paying bills, bringing incompletes to completion. And as each action was finished, something very deep began to emerge: how much I care about each part of my life, each person, each action. Sometimes I get going so fast that I forget to look back and savor the delights. Looking forward beckoned me to look back and notice all that is precious.

In asking myself the question, "Why Nepal?" another lesson came. The common greeting in Nepal is "Namasté" which translates to…

> I honor the place in you
> in which the entire universe dwells.
> I honor the place in you
> which is of love, of truth,
> of light and of peace.
> When you are in that place in you,
> and I am in that place in me,
> We are one.

Namasté is another way of saying what Wings stands for, a reverence for each individual and for the greater community. I want to spend time with people who live their appreciation for one another so simply and honestly. Perhaps that is why saying yes was and always will be worth the effort.

Reflections

1. What are some of the things you have dreamed of doing that you have told yourself you couldn't do?

2. What reasons did you use to convince yourself you couldn't do them? Impractical, time, money, what will others think, etc.?

3. When you dream dreams and don't do them, what is the impact on you and your life?

4. What is one thing you want to experience that you will take the risk to put yourself into 100 percent? When?

My perennial garden dedicated to my son, Matthew

Step into My Garden

Freedom has no bounds...
it grasps this experience of life,
but does not cling to it.
This precious gift of freedom
is our true spiritual essence,
and on its wings
we can soar magnificently within this
realm of wonder.

—Richard Oddo

16

Step into My Garden

March 1989

Have you ever watched a beautiful and abundant garden go untended? Watched as it slowly changed from a place of unsurpassed aliveness, symmetry, and color into a derelict place, uncared for…abandoned. Whenever I have watched this happen, I have felt a sense of sadness, for the garden and for the gardener. I've asked myself the question, "What could have happened that the gardener, who obviously cared so much, stopped caring?"

As a child, to answer the question, I created mysteries in my mind, conjuring up haunted houses and ghosts and things. As an adult, I have my own experience.

We live out of town and have a large garden, fifty by sixty feet, with an eight-foot deer fence and grass pathways that separate it into quarters and to make it easy to walk through. I used to spend almost my whole summer out there. First creating a blueprint, a design for where each flower and vegetable would grow best, and then digging, enriching the soil, planting, watering, watching things grow, and enjoying the harvest—wheelbarrows full, corn twelve feet tall! The flowers were a riot of color; I would cut armloads to bring into the house.

Our garden was a place where each of us could go and just be quiet, go and feel restored and a part of something magical. I can't tell you how many times the boys would disappear for a while and suddenly return with a green ring around their mouth from eating young onions, or holding a half eaten carrot in their hand, one more sweet crunchy bite. Or I would take my drawing things and sketch my thoughts for the next year's garden. Peaceful time-outs to feel the sun and watch the miracle of growing plants.

When our son, Matthew, died in 1986, we were devastated individually and as a family. Before his death, we did social things with our friends fairly often—dinners, playing games, going to the coast. Matt's death was the end of that. We didn't talk about it; we closed the door on our social life and stayed home. We closed the garden gate too and left our garden untended, we left it alone. It became a sad place. Unconsciously, we turned from friends and the garden and turned to each other, tending and nurturing each other and ourselves instead of working with the earth.

We began planting seeds of a different sort. The seeds of compassion and forgiveness, the seeds of letting go and loving unconditionally, the seeds of strength and vulnerability, tiny bits of life sustaining us. These seeds were watered with tears and nourished by long talks and silent hugs. These seeds have born the fruit of deeper love and respect than we ever knew was possible.

This summer, three years later, we planted a garden again. And instead of me being the main gardener, my husband, Kyle, is planting the seeds and watering. The garden is bursting into life again with the tending of his gentle hands. When I walk into the garden now, I feel many things. I feel the immediate delight of being in the midst of growing things. I feel proud of Kyle and touched by his nurturing. I feel inspired by the tenacity of life, stretching for the light. And I realize that is what we have been doing to heal—nurturing each other and stretching toward the light.

Remember my question, "What could have happened that the gardener, who obviously cared so much, stopped caring?" We never stopped caring for the garden; it is just that we cared so much for

Matthew and each other that all our energy went into our grieving, letting go, and healing. There was nothing left.

Standing in the fragrance of warm tomato vines, sweet peas, roses, and row upon row of growing things again, I hear the flowers and lettuces whispering that healing is a long and gentle process…be patient with yourself.

I am so grateful that I am surrounded by an abundant world where life springs forth eagerly when we tend our gardens and our spirits with care.

Won't you come into the garden? I would like my roses to see you.
—Richard B. Sheridan

Reflections

1. Looking back at your life, find a time when you stopped taking care of something that was important to you because something happened that deserved your complete attention. What deserved your full attention, and what did you stop doing?

2. What did you start doing to take care of your strongest priority?

3. What was the impact on your life?

4. Is there anything important for you to reclaim now?

Bhutanese grandma at festival, Thimpu

Destiny is not a matter of chance;
it is a matter of choice.
It is not a thing to be waited for,
it is a thing to be achieved.
            — William Jennings Bryan

17

Standing Tall

June 1990

I would like you to read this in a different manner than you usually do. Please either find a cooperative someone close at hand and ask them to read each paragraph to you slowly, or find a quiet spot and read this to yourself, one paragraph at a time, stopping often to let yourself imagine and wonder. I would like to give you the gift of a quiet moment with your creative self.

Settling down in your spot, let yourself become comfortable, your breathing becoming deep and regular, your body relaxing as you sit quietly, feeling yourself gently slowing down. It's okay for you to take a time-out. It's okay for you to relax. Breathing in is inspiring. Close your eyes and enjoy listening to the sound of your own breathing for several moments.

Feeling even more relaxed and comfortable now, gently begin to bring to mind the people you have held and hold in the highest respect, people who lived their lives in such a way that you felt inspired knowing them. Perhaps you would call them your heroes or your mentors, your friends. Beginning from the time you were a child, just as in a film, watch each one of your heroes and heroines come to life, moving, talking, doing the special things they did. Let the images of their faces come to mind, the way their eyes sparkled, the sound of their voices, the special words they said, perhaps even the feeling of the touch of their hand. Some of these people are people you know well and some you appreciated from afar, wishing you knew them.

As you watch each one, there is something else I would like you to become aware of, observing them closely. What was it about each one of them that made them so special to you? What qualities and traits do they have? What do you admire about each person? What do these special people stand for? As these qualities become clear to you, say the words aloud that describe them to you.

Listen to your own voice declare each person's uniqueness. Was it their integrity, their laugh, the way they were always there for you, the way they spoke the truth, the way they were involved with life? Could it have been the way they stood tall in the world, being themselves, their voices being heard, their love being shared? Were they bold enough to live in their own way? What was it? Become aware of what made them so special to you. As you think about these people, notice how you are feeling. Do you feel enriched just by thinking about them, inspired and comforted? Now take a moment to express your gratitude to each one for the contribution they made to your life.

Let's create a different picture now. What would your world have been like without these people? Notice how you feel even thinking about this loss. Gently looking back at your life, imagine what it would have been like without them to turn to, lean on, learn from, be loved by, and follow.

Sometimes we forget a very important part of the picture we are living inside of. We are so focused on looking outside of ourselves for direction, inspiration, solutions, stimulation, excitement, and leadership that we forget there are many people in the picture looking to us for those very same things.

Imagine that all of these people are back here with you now, standing around you and they are all eagerly looking at you. Their faces are full of anticipation, knowing that something important is about to happen. You are about to speak. What do you want to say to these respected people? Let yourself speak aloud, listening to your own words. And as you speak, notice if you are standing tall.

Reflections

1. How often do you really let yourself relax naturally, without using TV, books, computer, alcohol, drugs, etc., to do the job? What is more important than taking care of yourself?

2. Who are the people you hold with the highest respect and admiration, your heroes, heroines, mentors, your inspiration?

3. What qualities, traits, and behaviors made them so special to you?

4. What do you want these wonderful people to know about you? What do you want to say to them?

Children's cemetery monument, Kyoto, Japan

The Greatest Gift of All

When you are inspired by some great purpose,
some extraordinary project,
all your thoughts break their bonds.
Your mind transcends limitations,
your consciousness expands in every direction,
and you find yourself
in a new, great, and wonderful world.

—Yoga Sutras of Patanjali

18

The Greatest Gift of All

October 1990

Walking on the beach has always been one of the easiest ways for me to find my quiet self. Effortlessly moving along, one silent step after the other, gazing out at the endless ocean and sky, gives me a deep sense of my smallness and how I fit into my picture of life. Reflections, reveries, dreams, and visions float through my mind with the breeze, interrupted only by the call of a gull or a wave caressing my foot.

Walking today along the shore in the sparkling fall sunshine, my thoughts quieted, and then all of a sudden I was back in my first transformational education experience, the Personal Effectiveness Seminar in April 1982! The explosion of awareness and learning, of fun and laughter all poured back, along with the faces of so many new friends. Unfolding through my mind with each silent step, my continuation on through each seminar, being on teams, becoming an intern, working here, creating Wings Seminars with James, learning to be in partnership with James, and stepping into the role of leader, not really knowing what that meant.

As I "watched" my own unfolding and growth, I also saw the faces of all the people I have inter-

120

acted with as a student and as a teacher: teens, young people, older people, my family, and friends. One moment in each person's growth stood out over and over again, a moment so clear and sweet, a moment of profound realization and acceptance, a moment both peaceful and powerful. As I walked along, the wind whispered a name for this moment: "The greatest gift of all."

Yes, the greatest gift of all, the moment a person realizes and accepts that by extending themselves out into the world, they are instantly enriched and so is the world, that what they have to offer, simply by being themselves, is magnificent. There is a kind of amazement that goes with this moment too, amazement that the world is responsive to us. I had spent so many years thinking that I had nothing to offer anyone, nothing that anyone would want to hear nor would benefit from, that I held myself tightly within. I was certain that no one would ever want to spend time with me. I felt totally alone even when I was surrounded by people. Have you ever felt like that? It is a painful way to live, wanting to be part of and "knowing" it is not possible.

Walking along the beach and watching all your beautiful faces ignite in my mind, my own sense of gratitude and awe awakened. All of you who have come to Wings Seminars to learn and expand have not only enriched yourselves, you have enriched Wings, your family, your workplace, and every person that you have touched. Like the ripples in a pond when we toss a pebble in, all of you have touched your world gently and powerfully by being yourselves. This is the greatest gift of all, truly—being of the world, honestly and compassionately, extending ourselves out.

How often have you waited…waited for someone else to be the one to take the risk of initiating contact with you? How do you feel while you are waiting? Confident? Powerful? Desirable? No, I don't think so. More likely insufficient in some way, doubting your worth and capabilities.

To extend yourself, to initiate instead of waiting for someone to come find you, takes courage and a desire for meaningful relationships. When you extend yourself out to another, is there a possibility that they may not like it? Sure. There's also the possibility that they'll love it and you for risking.

So many people in this world would love to be loved by you, with a smile, a gentle word, a momentary easing of their loneliness, in thousands of simple ways. Is it time to stop waiting and start initiating what you want?

Perhaps this day, and maybe each day, you will choose to share the greatest gift of all: yourself.

Reflections

1. What have been pivotal learning experiences for you? How did you change your life as a result?

2. Have you experienced "the greatest gift of all," accepting that who you are and what you have to offer is magnificent? And that by extending yourself out into the world that both you and the world are enriched?

3. What keeps you waiting for someone to come find you? How do you feel while you are waiting?

4. What are some simple things you could do today to initiate respectful and compassionate connection with others?

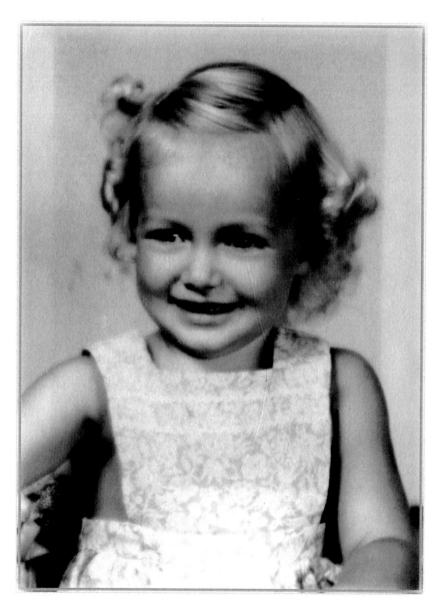

Me at around two years

Dreams Do Come True

The only way to discover
the limits of the possible
is to go beyond them
into the impossible.
—Arthur C. Clarke,
Profiles of the Future

19

Dreams Do Come True

November 1991

When I was a child, I had many dreams, dreams that seemed more real to me than what happened every day, day in and day out. I dreamed of being a garbage man (we didn't have "persons" yet, and I did want to be a man!), of being the first girl president, of being a ballerina, a teacher, a wizard, an actress, a backup singer for Diana Ross, and much more! My dreams were a veritable cast of thousands. You name it, I had dreams about it. I remember waking up in the morning, sometimes exhausted by my nighttime life of dreaming, having gone many places and done different and sometimes dangerously exciting things.

My life truly seemed to be on two different planes. This wasn't strange to me; it felt completely natural that my whole life, night and day, would be vital and exciting. My friends and I talked about our dreams and similar things happened for them too.

Somewhere around twelve or thirteen, my dreams started to change. As I became aware of what being a responsible adult meant, my dreams became more serious and not nearly as refreshing as before. I paid less attention to my dreams, finding them serious and demanding. I dreamed less and less as my confusion about becoming an adult increased.

Choosing what I wanted to do with my life became a very difficult decision-making process rather than a choice based in dreams and passion. After much investigation, I've found this is true for many people. Does this sound familiar to you?

What I have come to realize is that my early dreams were a kind of practice, trying on different ways of being to see what I really wanted "to become." My adolescent confusion was based in thinking how I felt about myself and my life was all dependent on what I "did." Constrictive dreaming is living out our fears, great and small, of not being enough, of doing or having terrible things done to us—the night terrors! The deeper realization now emerging is that what we yearn for and dream about is an ideal state of being, a way of feeling about life and ourselves that we make real through choices and actions.

Our dreams do come true. When our dreams are heavy and confusing, so is our life; when our dreams are stimulating and uplifting, so is our life. When we turn our backs on inspiration, we create lives of desolation.

Expansive dreaming is simply a process of allowing…allowing our own best self speak to us of all we are capable of giving and being, of tasting and feeling, and of the grand adventures that call to us to be a part of this magnificent world. Expansive dreaming is embracing our lives wholeheartedly; living is making our dreams come true.

When you go to sleep tonight, remember to dream expansively.

> The greatest achievement was at first and for a time a dream.
> The oak sleeps in the acorn;
> the bird waits in the egg;
> and in the highest vision of the soul,
> a waking angel stirs.
> Dreams are the seedlings of realities.

Your circumstances may be uncongenial,
but they shall not long remain so
if you but perceive an Ideal and strive to
reach it.
You cannot travel within and stand still without…
He who cherishes a beautiful vision,
a lofty ideal in his heart,
will one day realize it.
—James Allen, *As a Man Thinketh*

Reflections

1. When you were a kid growing up, what were some of your dreams about what you wanted to be and do?

2. Which dreams were most compelling? And what was it about each one that was so attractive to you?

3. When did you let go of childhood dreams and start being more practical, more like an adult? What was the impact?

4. What are your dreams for your life now? Are you living them? What is the impact?

Butterfly at work, Bhutan

Spreading Our Wings

*The journey is to be
your unique, specific self,
who will only exist once in this
universe, able to do and be
what no one else
can do and be.*

— Robert P. Crosby

20

Spreading Our Wings

March 1992

On March 2, 1992, filled with excitement and curiosity, I boarded United Airlines flight 158, a fifteen-hour, nonstop flight across the Pacific Ocean. The plane was filled to capacity with Asians going home and a polyglot of multinationals heading for one of the biggest crossroads in the world, Hong Kong! Just hearing all the different languages spoken amongst the passengers was thrilling! I grew up with airplanes in my blood (my dad was a captain for Pan Am, my brother was a captain for Pan Am and United, and both my sister and I were flight attendants for Pan Am a long time ago!). I felt delighted to be on a 747 again starting a new adventure.

Why Hong Kong? Because Wings was asked to present our seminars there, and I got to go first. What an opportunity! The essence of my personal vision is to live my dreams and to assist others to live theirs. Here was an opportunity to have the people assisted be from many cultures, my global vision. To step into another culture, to teach, to assist people to open to their own magnificence and personal power and then for them to go share their learning with their families, co-workers, and community…this excites me.

When I sat down in my seat, I knew that I had everything I needed: my seminar outline, music, clothes, a huge amount of loving support from family, interns, and staff, and total self-trust that whatever I did would be the best I knew how to give. I felt like a pioneer, setting off for the unknown as well prepared as possible and knowing that anything could happen—a true adventure.

So many incredible things happened! Simply walking down the street at noon, noticing commerce in action, the smells, tastes, and textures of this multinational city, was a learning experience. Teaching in the elegant Hong Kong Convention Center, which sits at the edge of Hong Kong Harbor, watching forty-three participants from eleven different nations open their hearts and minds to love and accountability was inspiring. Meeting so many people who care about the quality of life in our world, who will open their minds to new learning and take action to change things, filled me with a sense of deep common purpose, desire, and hope. *Hope!*

My Hong Kong adventure beckoned me to learn about my world and myself. It made it very clear to me that people all over the world are thirsty for love and a meaningful life. People want to be their best selves, to feel inspired and valuable in their daily lives, to experience a peaceful and loving world that begins inside of them. People want their children to be safe, loved, well educated, and capable of creating meaningful and fulfilling lives. I was so touched to hear each person from such varied backgrounds say they wanted the same things. I learned from experience that, given the opportunity and an encouraging and supportive learning environment, people rise to the greatest heights and bring others along.

What great adventure is awaiting you? Calling to you so that you can expand your vision of yourself and your world? What do you want to contribute to this great big beautiful world and all its people? When you look back at your long and healthy life, how do you want to be remembered, your legacy? All this starts with a dream.

"Twenty years from now, you will be more disappointed by the things that you didn't do than by the ones you did do. So throw off the bowlines. Sail away from the safe harbor. Catch the trade winds in your sails. Explore. Dream. Discover" (Mark Twain).

Is it time to spread your wings?

1. What do you want to contribute to this great, big, beautiful world and all its people?

2. What gifts and talents do you possess that you are not using? How do you feel when you are not using your abilities?

3. When you look back at your long and healthy life, how do you want to be remembered?

4. What is your legacy?

Fanciful garden oil painting by my niece Kristin Twigg

Taking Tea with Adversity

It's not what we do, but the peace with which we do it, that contributes to the world.

—Hugh Prather

21

Taking Tea with Adversity

May 1992

Oh, the world is full of wondrous lessons that keep us on our toes. Oftentimes we have no idea that what's happening is an opportunity to learn, because many of these lessons are ushered into our lives by resistance or adversity!

For example: an event takes place, we look at it, interpret the event as adversity, a misfortune, or a setback, and then we decide it is worthy of a negative response. So we resist, defend, or fight. Now, mind you, all of this happens in the twinkling of an eye. This is not a conscious response, it is a reactive, unconscious response based on our belief system and past experiences.

While we are resisting, we are gathering all pertinent information to back up the rightness of our decision to resist. We are culling the archives of our past experiences, so we can justify ourselves to others if they question our behavior when we denounce or fight back. We may even try to get others to join us in the resistance, allies to bolster the strength of our defense. Does this sound familiar to you? It is the age-old pattern of reactivity, defense, and thinking we are right, which means they are wrong.

Much harm has come to the world through this pattern of reacting to perceived adversity: big-otry, abuse, broken relationships, misuse of power, polarized communities, and in the extreme, war. Some good has come from it too: high ideals represented, just causes becoming recognized. Yet when people standing up for "just causes" make the "other side" sound mindless, evil, stupid, you name it, it only causes more polarization, a breakdown of communication, and diminishes the possibility of common ground or community. In my mind, the harm done far outweighs the good.

Is it natural to resist, to be afraid of the unknown, the different, and the foreign? Sure. It is a defense mechanism to keep us safe and whole, heralding back to the time of the woolly mammoth and survival. But just because we have the feeling of adversity or resistance doesn't mean we "have to" attack or defend ourselves. Am I saying to stand back and do nothing? Absolutely not! Having the truth be known is vital to our growth as human beings. So what to do, especially when you care?

At approximately 4:00 p.m. each day, the British take tea. A long-standing tradition, teatime is an oasis in the day, a time to sit and relax, to refresh themselves after the industrious part of the day is done, and to enjoy friendship and gracious conversation. It is a peaceful time-out.

When a lesson comes waltzing into our lives with resistance as its partner, or an event occurs and we feel the desire to resist or defend, what would it be like if we took a nice deep breath, paused until we felt calm, and then said,

"Pull up a chair, let us take tea together. Let us take some time to explore and be curious, being respectful of each other while being responsible for our own thoughts, feelings, and actions. Let's have a peaceful time-out."

Instead of reacting, we get curious about the other person and their intentions as well as our own. We open our mind and heart instead of having our hackles come up and our lips turn into a sneer, looking for the jugular and wanting to prove that we are right. Some of my greatest learning has come from checking out my assumptions about the truth, by asking instead of telling, and discovering that my assumptions were not true at all.

So often it seems we forget the things that are most important to us. We want to feel peaceful, and yet we don't. Choosing peace is a skill, a discipline, and a delight! And choosing peace is our gift to ourselves and the world.

Take tea with adversity; listen, learn, and then choose peace.

Reflections

1. What are the things about yourself that you react to most strongly (e.g., needing to be right when your thoughts are challenged, feeling hurt if you don't get what you want)?

2. What are your patterns of reactivity (e.g., the silent treatment, arguing, isolating, addictions)?

3. What is the impact in your relationships and on you?

4. What is one new behavior you will do that will give you healthier results?

Young monks at play with David Larson, Bhutan

Dream as if you'll live forever.
Live as if you'll die today.
—James Dean

22

Being Your Own Best Friend

August 1992

Have you ever imagined what it would be like to have a very best friend? If you could magically create one, what would they be like? Someone who listened to you attentively, respected your opinions, told you the truth in such a way that you loved to hear it? Someone who loved you so much they wanted only the best for you, laughed with you, and shared themselves delightfully? Someone you could be quiet with and yet connected to? If you could have anything you want, what qualities would you choose and value most in your best friend?

If this person were to suddenly walk into your life today, now, what would happen, how would things change? How would you feel? What kinds of things would you want to do together? How would your life expand?

You know, we do seem to hope a lot for someone else to come along and make us feel good, don't we? And when they don't do it right, we get pretty upset. It's taken me a long time to realize that the quality of the relationship I have with myself determines not only the quality of my relationships with others but the quality of my life itself.

When I was growing up, I had no idea that I could possibly be my own best friend. If I had talked like that or even felt like that, my friends would have laughed at me and thought me extremely weird. I wish I had known being my own best friend was possible back then. I would have had a lot less heartache than I did. I remember looking out the window with longing as a kid, seeing my friends together outside and thinking, "Why aren't I with them?" I wasn't with them because I was waiting for them to come find me, a strange kind of hide-and-seek that they didn't know I was playing.

Do you remember ever thinking your were left out and feeling lonely? How did you manage those thoughts and feelings? I remember saying to myself, "I don't care!" even though I cared very much. I also pretended that I was very involved with something much more important than my friends so they wouldn't see my hurt. Time went by, and my ways of compensating became the norm; now I held people away, thinking I was independent. And I was so lonely inside.

Then I took the Personal Effectiveness Seminar and realized that being my own best friend is actually my job, my responsibility. The ball is in my court. How I feel inside is my own creation. I am so fortunate I learned this at Wings. I am more than fortunate, I am ecstatic, because Wings is a place where people of all shapes, sizes, ages, backgrounds, etc., are learning to be their own best friend. Wings is here to assist you, to support you in being your own best friend and knowing how to create fulfilling and rewarding relationships in all aspects of your life!!

Learning to be your own best friend takes commitment in the deepest, purest sense to yourself…to living your life and valuing it as a unique creation. I share this poem with you to help you remember to be your own best friend.

mighty guest of merely me
traveler from eternity;
in a single wish, receive
all i am and dream and have.
Be thou gay by dark and day;
gay as only truth is gay
(nothing's false, in earth in air
in water and in fire, but fear—
mind's a coward; lies are laws)
laugh, and make each no thy yes:
love; and give because the why
—gracious wanderer, be thou gay
                    —E. E. Cummings

Reflections

1. Do you remember ever thinking you were left out as a kid and feeling lonely? Whose attention did you want?

2. How did you manage those thoughts and feelings? What did you do?

3. If you could have anything you want, what qualities would you choose and value most in your best friend?

4. What is it going to take for you to be those things to yourself, to be your own best friend?

Festival dancer telling a story through movement, Bhutan

Breaking Out of the Box!

*Imagination is more important
than knowledge,
for knowledge is limited,
whereas imagination embraces
the entire world.*

—Albert Einstein

23

Breaking Out of the Box!

October 1992

The Wings logo is very significant to me and our organization. It signifies leaving the confines of established limitations and exploring new territory. In other words, breaking out of the box.

On October 1, James and I signed an agreement that ends our seven-year partnership in Wings, an agreement that assists both of us to move beyond the confines of our established limits and to explore new territory. Something valued, cherished, and known is ending: our partnership. As I write, I am filled with paradoxical emotions like sadness, worry, fear, and my old friend self-doubt. On the other hand, I am feeling exhilaration, excitement, amazement at my own courage, pride, gratitude, curiosity, freedom—in other words, expansiveness!

How did all of this come about? This spring when I was travelling to Hong Kong, I had time to look at Wings from a different perspective, what we call fresh eyes. I realized that in our partnership, both James and I were holding ourselves back from our true potential. We had fallen into patterns that worked well and yet limited us both (does this sound familiar?). I decided to give this realization some time, being the cautious creature I am. I also began exploring what I really want in life, what my dreams are—in other words, my own personal vision.

In August, the pieces fell into place. I became crystal clear about what I want. It was time to talk with James. Even though I was crystal clear, it took every ounce of courage I had to say what I knew to be true. I was afraid of all sorts of things—hurting James, being selfish, not being right, etc.—but mainly I was afraid of two things. First was breaking up the established order. And secondly, taking ownership 100 percent of what I want.

I did it anyway. As I spoke, heart pounding, perspiration gathering, throat dry, I noticed that James was not responding the way I had anticipated (upset, taken aback, hurt, angry); he was nodding his head in agreement! Amazement! All this anxiety, and he's in agreement with me. Wow!

We had a great conversation about our dreams, what we want for Wings and for each other. We both realized it was time for positive change and exploration of new territory. As our agreement grew, we decided to create a context for the transformation we and Wings would be going through.

We agreed that practicing what we teach was essential in everything we did:

1. Win-win. Wings as a corporation, our participants, our staff, Kris, and James would all benefit by whatever we decided
2. We would be completely honest with each other
3. Our love for each other would be nourished throughout the process

Guess what? We did it!

Wings Seminars goes on, offering you and your family and friends the very best seminars in the Northwest, perhaps the entire country. I am free in Wings to implement changes that are so important to me, and James is free to explore new territory. It took some time to work it all out, and we did it!

I am so proud of James; his heart and commitment have been so apparent through this whole time (and his playfulness is back!). I am so thankful to Jessie Reeder for her selfless wisdom and assistance. I am so blessed to have a staff that holds this work and Wings in such high esteem that they consistently give their best and tell the truth.

And I am proud of me too!

What I have learned, once again, is that it may be scary to dream, to change direction, to tell the truth, to stand up for what you believe in, to end things. And it is essential if you want to find out more about who you are. Breaking out of the box right now is the most exciting thing Wings has done in quite a while!

I thank you for the support you have given Wings in the past and hope that you will allow us to provide you with the best seminars available in the future. That's what we are here for. What box are you ready to break out of?

Reflections

1. Before making a change in something important to you, what fears arise?

2. When you are fearful, how do you handle it? What behaviors do you do, what thoughts run through your mind?

3. Where are the places in your life that you most want to create positive change?

4. Write down specifically the outcomes you want to create and your first action steps to get you started.

Heart shaped leaf, Bhutan

You cannot do a kindness too soon,
for you never know how soon
it will be too late.
                    —Ralph Waldo Emerson

24

Love Letters Straight from the Heart

December 1992

It's that time of year when we start thinking of gift giving to those closest and dearest to us, of feasts and celebrations, Hanukkah, Christmas, and the celebration of winter solstice. It's a time of gathering those we love the most, of laughing with them, of noticing the very best in them (sometimes difficult to do at a family gathering!), and of celebrating ancient spiritual and religious traditions and the great abundance we all share by exchanging gifts and preparing sumptuous meals. Sounds great, and yet… Is there something missing? During this season of celebration, do you feel filled up or perhaps empty? There sure is a lot of emphasis on the *spirit* of the season. Where does the spirit come from, and when does it arrive?

In case you are in doubt, I love the trappings and history of Christmas, the traditions that have arisen since approximately 336 AD when Christmas was first celebrated. I deeply respect the Jewish celebration of the victory of the Maccabees over Antiochus IV Epiphanes in 165 BC—Hanukkah.

Winter solstice is an ancient celebration of being happy and thankful to be alive as the days become longer and of sharing stored abundance. All are long-established and meaningful celebrations of spiritual freedom and hope for humanity. The spirit of these traditional holy days is laden with joy, love, pride, acceptance, shared abundance, reverence for life, and peace. How do we bring the spirit back if we do not feel it?

So often as I walk through shops and grocery stores looking at the faces of people as they prepare for the holidays, I feel sad that I see so little joy and very little of the glow that I associate with peace. As I walk, I wonder what each person's life is like and if there is any way I can brighten their day. A smile, a nod, and I am gone. What else?

What would happen if that father of three toddlers or that teenage beauty were to go back to their car and find a letter on the windshield addressed simply "To you." They may be impatient as they open it, maybe wondering what kind of come-on this is, and then they read the words in my handwriting.

"You are no different than any person on this earth, and you are…you are light and truth and humor and love and beauty. You are endless and timeless. I do not know you, and yet I do. I love you in this precious moment of this thing we call time. We are travelling through time together, even though you do not know me. I honor how you are caring for those you love, especially yourself. I feel your pain and separation, and I delight in your joy. My life is enriched knowing there are people like you in our world. The greatest gift you have to offer is you.

Thank you for being simply you. With love, all things are possible."

Any number of things could happen. Hopefully, one of them being the person would know that someone cared and wished to send a message of love and acknowledgment, a love letter straight from the heart.

Imagine going into an airport, opening the phone book, choosing a name, or several names, and writing a love letter straight from the heart, mailing it, and hopping on your plane. Imagine choosing a distant family member, or even one who is close, and sharing your thoughtful words. Imagine sending your words of peace and love out into the world, your own words, words that speak to your soul. Unconditional caring and giving—isn't that what we all want to experience? And yet so often we wait for another to initiate, to come find us. Please stop waiting and start loving.

I think I have just created a new tradition for myself that takes me back to the spirit of our ancient traditions. It brings back the feeling of holy days into my everyday life.

Will you join me, at least once? When we look for ways to love and acknowledge, that's usually what we find. And when we share them with the world, our world is rich with meaning.

How would you feel if you received a love letter straight from the heart? Write it and give it away now.

Reflections

1. What traditions do you practice to celebrate the abundance in your life (e.g., Christmas, Hanukkah, Solstice, other)?

2. How are the things you do fulfilling and meaningful for you? How are they stressful, perhaps draining?

3. Painting a new picture of how you want to celebrate, what will you do differently?

4. Who do you think would want to receive a love letter straight from the heart from you?

Audacious Wings Intern Group, 2005–2006

Choosing Service

*I have found that among its other benefits,
giving liberates the soul of the giver.*

— Maya Angelou

25

Choosing Service

Growing up in the forties, fifties, and sixties, I mostly learned about service through osmosis by watching my parents, the people in my neighborhood and at church, and watching *Victory at Sea* on television. I had Lutheran, community, and military ideas about what it was. The way I interpreted these messages was that it was very important to relieve the suffering of others and it could come at a big price—your life.

My biggest heroes at the time, Jesus, Gandhi, Martin Luther King Jr., and JFK, were visionaries wanting to create a better world, and they were all assassinated. Would that happen to me too if I had a dream and helped make the world a better place? You may think this silly, even ridiculous, and yet it made perfect sense to me.

I also saw another aspect of service that was upsetting to me. I would overhear the ladies at church, my Grandma Inga, the elders of my church, and my teachers at school expressing resentment, frustration, and even anger if they were not appreciated the way they thought they should be. Adding these two things together, I became suspicious of people's motivations and the value of being in service.

All of this changed when I started participating in this work and then choosing it as my life's work. I began to see and experience the beauty and generosity of choosing service and what the words "unconditional giving" mean.

As I talk with you about service now, it is very important to understand a distinction I draw. The historical definition of service is focused outward and has to do with being helpful, dutiful, and tirelessly providing for others, even to the extent of personal loss or suffering. Now, that sounds extreme, and yet to some people that is what service is about: sacrifice. When we talk about service at Wings, it is a balance of in focus and out focus. Sharing yourself unconditionally with others, your talents, capabilities, and heart, being an instrument of kindness and caring, all the while taking care of yourself.

Wings' mission is to inspire and support positive change, creating an abundant, loving, and respectful world community. And one of the main ways we do that is by being dedicated to service. Every day at Wings, we create an environment that is rich in respect, compassion, creativity, honesty, playfulness, acceptance, risk-taking, and community. In many ways, we have created family in the healthiest form. This does not just happen! It is not an accident. My staff and I hold our day-to-day working and living environment as crucial to the integrity of our vision for Wings.

Service is an invitation to celebrate what you have to contribute and who you are! Giving to others is a way that touches the world gently with love and respect.

Choosing service is an acknowledgement that we have something of value to share—our energy, love, expertise, time, and sometimes simply our calm presence—listening to and holding the person we are with as valuable and important.

Service is choosing to be fully present in each moment using what we have been given for the highest good for ourselves and others.

Do you want to share your love, capabilities, and enthusiasm? How would you, your family, your workplace, your community, your place of worship, the children of the world benefit by you stepping into an even higher level of being in service in your life? The world community is thirsty for the calm presence of service, for the very gifts and talents you have to share in abundance.

There is a very dedicated and tireless group of individuals that I watch transform their lives through service over a period of a year: the Wings Leadership interns. They give of themselves joyfully and patiently, with tremendous enthusiasm and playfulness. As I work with them as a group and as individuals, I am awed by their incredible commitment to living life as whole, happy, contributing people while helping others. Believe it or not, since I started in the first intern group in 1983, there have been hundreds of interns!

Each day I feel deeply honored and thankful that I "get to be" involved with so many people who support Wings' vision, doing simple things with great love, presence, and service. Thinking about creating a better world is one thing; taking action to create it is another, because action takes commitment and courage.

I am thankful for every person on this earth who chooses service now.

Reflections

1. How did you learn about being in service?

2. What were the strong, healthy aspects of service and what were the negative ones?

3. What is your definition of service now?

4. Who is someone who models your definition? How do you feel when you are with them?

5. If you could do one thing for the world, what would it be?

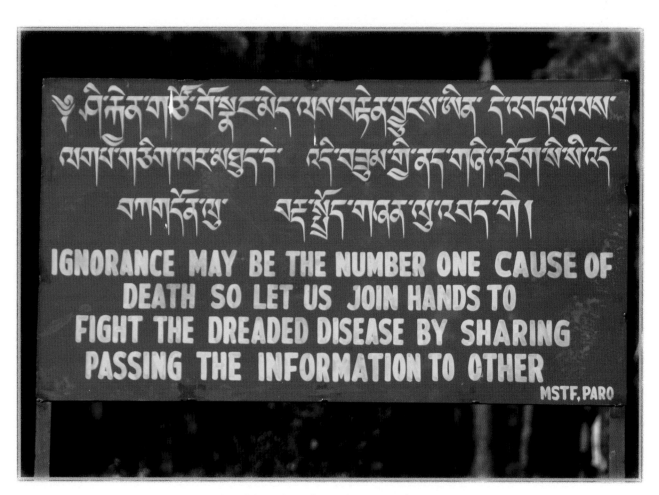

Inspiring sign along the way, Bhutan

A promise has real power.
A promise made from a stand
that who you are is your word,
engages you as a participant.
You cease to be a spectator,
and your words become actions
that actually impact the world.

— Werner Erhard

26

Pass It On

Have you ever had such a great experience that you were just bursting to share it with someone, overflowing with excitement and enthusiasm, wanting everyone you know to have the same experience? Perhaps an exceptional meal in a little-known restaurant, a trip to a foreign country, watching a must-see film, a breathtaking adventure in nature, reading a new author's work, a spiritual insight that leaves you tingling, discovering a political candidate you can finally believe in—so many possibilities.

What do you want to do in those moments? Perhaps silently savor your experience to its fullest, gleaning every morsel of meaning and nuance, or maybe jump up and down with sheer delight wanting to shout out your joy, "Amazing!" What a wide range we all have to express our deepest feelings. At some point in time, I think we want to share the impact of those moments with the people we care most about.

Throughout my life, whenever I discovered something that I thought was exceptional, or had an experience that opened doors in my heart and mind, I would pass on the information to whomever I thought would benefit from it. It seemed only natural to do this. I thought that if everyone was doing this, being a free economy and a free society, soon the level of excellence and meaning all around the world would go up, because people would be supporting goods, services, and experiences of the highest quality.

My enthusiasm for quality was my guide. My desire to have everyone experiencing the best life has to offer was my motivation.

I didn't know until 1982, when I did the Personal Effectiveness Seminar, that what I was doing was called advocacy. I just did it because I wanted to. Advocacy means to speak or write in favor of something publicly or to support something you value.

It has been easy for me to advocate when it has been about goods and services, because I knew people would probably like what I advocated for; I am a good judge of quality. Where it got tough was when I thought the other person would not agree with me. I would talk about what was "safe," where I would not experience any resistance. I realized in some areas of my life, I was a "sunshine advocate." I'd advocate only for the things I knew people would agree with me on.

This insight was deeply disturbing and uncomfortable. The people I most admire are the ones who have had the courage to advocate for things that are deeply important to them even when others do not agree. People who stood and said basically, "There's an elephant in the living room!" I was playing it safe to be accepted, afraid to rock the boat and stand up for things that I thought were exceptional. This affected every part of my life, the way I parented, participated at work, even the smallest things like which movies I would talk about! My self-judgment was, "*gutless*!" And I didn't like it one bit.

So I started exploring how I could stand up for what I believe in no matter what the circumstances. Even if my heart is pounding out of my chest, my mouth dry as the desert, and sweat is running down my sides, I want to express my message in a way that others can hear and understand. Not only my truth, but also my passion, my humanity, and my vision of what's possible.

I started in a small way at home with my husband and my children and was amazed at how much easier it was than I anticipated. After building my self trust through practice at home, I started advocating honestly and authentically with my friends. I was encouraged by how the quality of my relationships grew and deepened.

Over time I discovered three important things.

When I am:

1. being authentic and honest about what I am advocating for,

2. sharing information clearly and enthusiastically,

3. respectful of the person I am talking with, which means my intention is to create the highest good,

IT WORKS!

What do you care about passionately that you are ready to pass on?

Reflections

1. Looking back over time, what are things that you have cared about deeply and not told anyone about?

2. What were your reasons for keeping them private?

3. What do you think about people who respectfully reveal what they care about and think is important? How do you feel in their presence?

4. What do you care enough about to risk advocating, passing it on?

Cathy Tronquet capturing the glory of prayer flags, Bhutan

Taking Care of Yourself vs. Taking Good Care of Yourself

*I am listening to the river
as it speaks my name.
I am feeling fully present
as I aim,
…To reach the stars,
…To pierce the void,
I am listening.*

— *Kris King*

27

Taking Care of Yourself vs. Taking Good Care of Yourself

April 1993

Over the past year, I have been dealing with a number of major life situations, like realizing that my business partner and I wanted different and conflicting things and collaborating on ending our business relationship in a way that we both felt respected and loved; deciding if it is time to go into new markets; having my teenage son drop out of school; being financially stretched and stressed; taking on full responsibility for fulfilling my own dreams; and to top it all off, realizing that I'm almost a third of the way through life! I say a third because I want to live to be at least 157 (the year 2100—I want to see what it's like), and on May 9, I will turn 50. (Yes, please, I know I'm loved when I receive birthday cards!)

During all this time, I thought I was taking good care of myself, doing what I needed to do to stay not only sane but healthy too. Well, one of my favorite quotes is, "An unexamined life is not worth living" (Socrates), and as I started to examine this past year, I had a major insight that I would like to share with you.

Yes, every single one of the life situations that I've worked with this year has been resolved in a way that aligns with my deepest values, and I am proud of the results I have created with the help of all those involved. However, one of the side effects is that I've gained ten pounds!

As I look back, I realize that I used food to soften the edges of my fear and stress, to feel peaceful for a while. I used food to comfort and reward myself for all my hard work, telling myself that I deserved the extra indulgence. I used food to deny feeling out of control, not knowing how things would turn out. I had been taking care of myself by eating to stay calm and grounded. I didn't plan it or think about it, I just did it unconsciously and now I realize *it has been a pattern all my life.*

So was I really taking good care of my "self"? As I stayed with the question, not judging or thrashing myself, just open to information, this is what I learned.

My unconscious found a way to slow me down while my conscious mind was deeply focused on survival during change and going a million miles an hour. There were times when what and how I was eating came into my consciousness, I noticed it, and because my other demands were so strong, I dismissed the awareness. Besides eating unconsciously, I stopped taking the time to walk each day. Other things seemed more important.

As I look back, I wonder what would have happened if instead of taking care of my "self" unconsciously, I had done it consciously. And what I see is, I would have *taken good care* of myself. If I had made my health and well-being as high a priority as the other things that were happening, I would have eaten more consciously and found other ways to slow down and ground myself. I would have taken the time to go walking each morning to move my body and clear the cobwebs out of my brain. The only judgment I have of myself in all of this, is wondering when I'm going to remember that my physical, mental, emotional, and spiritual well-being are as important as finishing a task on time, and that one need not suffer because of the other. If my intention is to create healthy balance in my life, I will.

Now that I've had my time to reflect and realize, I can move from unconscious ways to care for myself to healthy, conscious ways to take good care of myself. What a miracle awareness is!

Asking ourselves the right questions and listening to our answers without judgment is taking good care of ourselves too.

So when will I remember that my well-being is actually more important than the task at hand? Definitely now.

How about you?

Reflections

1. Looking back over past events, in times of stress, what have you done to take care of yourself that has had negative consequences?

2. When you realized what you were doing to yourself, how did you feel? And what did you do?

3. What are some new behaviors you can do consciously that will take good care of yourself?

Lustrous Wangdue lilies, Bhutan

What Happened to Joy?

*The real voyage of discovery
consists not in seeking new landscapes
but in having new eyes.*

　　　　　　　　　　—Marcel Proust

28

What Happened to Joy?

May 1993

Since beginning this work in 1982, I have noticed a cultural pattern that disturbs me greatly, and one that I think is having a profoundly negative impact at the conscious and unconscious level. I have noticed that it's much more acceptable to have a problem or many problems, or to be depressed than it is to be excited, joyful, delighted, and glowing with beauty and health.

There are so many signs, subtle and blatant, that signify this preference. People who are needy, see themselves as taken advantage of by someone more powerful than they, or victimized get lots of attention, sympathy, and supportive conversation. People who are enthusiastic and self-reliant, who can take care of themselves, get very little. As a matter of fact, very often someone who is excited and filled with joy is blatantly judged as being phony or trying "to pull the wool over our eyes." Suspicion, doubt, and the fear of "being taken for a ride" often follow someone who feels good and looks happy!

What happened to joy? Why this apprehension or taking down a notch of happy people? I could give you a couple hundred historical reasons, but so what. All that would create is an understanding of why we are messed up in our priorities. And we are! We live in the midst of a world that is both good and bad, perfect and imperfect, and everything in between. We live in a country that is one of the richest in the world with freedom of choice, and yet we seem to be in a constant grieving process for what we don't have!

In my travels to Nepal, Bhutan, and Thailand over the years, I have seen some of the deepest economic poverty imaginable. In 1989, when I first traveled from the airport in Kathmandu to our hotel, I was in tears seeing children with distended stomachs, flies circling their eyes, and filth in the street. My heart was breaking. It took me two days to see that those same children were smiling and laughing, holding each other's hands, and taking care of each other. They were strong and healthy in body, and with so little they were rich in spirit and love.

Joy is the feeling of great pleasure and delight, elation! Enthusiasm means to be filled with God, inspired. Both are signs of the light and life energy within each one of us. You may have noticed, the more you focus on what you don't want, the more you create it and all the feelings that go with it—anger, resentment, frustration…poverty. Our world will always be filled with paradox and things we do not understand or agree with, even things we hate. Does that mean that we cannot be joyful? No.

Our most important question is not, "Why do I deny my joy?" It is, "How do I deny my joy?" How do I miss the things in my life that are filled with joy? By not looking for them! Dr. Martin Seligman said, "Careful research shows that people with pessimistic habits of thinking can transform mere setbacks into disasters." We spend so much time looking for what's missing, what's wrong, that we forget to be grateful for what is present! We are surrounded by beauty in every moment, nature, the human spirit, and many times all we see is the stain on the carpet at our feet.

We have good reason to choose joy. It's healthy, it feels good, and it's contagious! Laugh and your immune system is strengthened. Dance and your body is washed with endorphins. Play and you feel like a child, resourceful, creative, and spunky. There is research data that now suggests that happy people, in general, live longer, more meaningful lives.

The first step to joy is appreciation, seeing value in the smallest things and even the most difficult things. The second step is gratitude, being thankful for the experiences life offers us. The third step is the decision to use everything in life as a tool for learning and expanding consciousness. Each step is a powerful shift in perspective from scarcity to abundance.

When we open to the positive, more and more keeps rolling in! What happened to joy? Nothing. Maybe it's time to remember it, to look with new eyes at all there is to be grateful for and to allow joy to fill your being.

Reflections

1. What happens for you when you listen to someone tell their story of being mistreated or taken advantage of at work, at home, and in relationships?

2. Have you ever thought you were being judged for expressing your joy and playfulness? What did you do in response?

3. How do you deny yourself joy? What thoughts, feelings, and behaviors?

4. How are you going to use steps 1–3 to bring more joy into your life?

Doorways of Bhutan

Endings and Beginnings

Blaze a trail
with your heart,
Listen to the music
of your soul,
And fly!

—Kris King

29

Endings and Beginnings

June 1993

Endings have not always been easy times for me, and after being involved with so many people over the years, I know this is true for most people.

Have you ever known someone who never finished their doctorate? Or someone who stayed in a destructive relationship for years and years, someone who never really left home, or someone who grieved a loss for years and years and never let go? Or someone who was so terrified of death that they didn't really live? Each person tenaciously held on to an existing experience, even if it was over or lacking in richness or substance, because they were afraid of letting go, of what could happen next.

Two of the most significant endings in my life were having breast cancer in 1979 at thirty-six, which ended my body as whole, and the death of my son, Matthew, in 1986 a week after his twenty-first birthday, which ended our profound mother and son relationship. Both were breath-taking and gut-wrenching experiences that I have molded my life with and that molded me. The thoughts about cancer and death that I had before they became realities terrified me and confused me. When I was actually experiencing them, it wasn't that way at all. I had crossed a threshold, from illusion to reality.

Endings signify so many different things to each of us, from death and destruction, abandonment and failure to freedom and self-acknowledgement, achievement and creativity. What is the difference that lets one person see terror in an ending and another see excitement and learning?

The difference for me came when I realized I didn't have to be scared or terrified like I had seen in the movies or read about in books, that cancer and death don't have to be about tragic endings. With the help of a lot of loving and patient people, I started to believe in life again and my ability to choose life passionately in each moment. My cancer became a beginning of my strength. Matthew's death became the beginning of my faith. Basically, I moved from fear of loss to acceptance of life.

Think of the people in your life who you have seen transform their fear of an ending into a new beginning in how they thought and interacted, basically lived their lives. I have witnessed many such miracles over the years. Valiant, courageous, and even playful engagements with adversity, divorce, illness, and death. Each person an inspiration because of how they use the ending to fuel their own spiritual growth and learning. They take an ending and make it a beginning. What an inspiration to us to live each moment here and now. After all, what are we waiting for?

After Matthew died, this thought came into my mind. It helps me trust life and reminds me to choose life.

> Every exit
> is an entrance
> to somewhere else.
> —Kris King

Every time a completion occurs, the next moment is the beginning of something new. Instead of looking backward at where we have come from, this is a reminder to notice where we are and what we are going toward. Letting go of the past with deep appreciation and opening to what lies ahead with curiosity and courage.

The difference that makes a difference? Yes!

Reflections

1. What have been the most significant endings in your life? Describe them fully.

2. What did you learn about yourself in each?

3. Have you resisted letting something come to a natural ending? What were the consequences?

4. What do you want to begin? What are you curious about and courageous enough to pursue with all your heart?

Happy Bhutanese woman with new glasses and a Polaroid photo!

I wish I could show you,
When you are lonely or in darkness
The Astonishing Light
Of your own Being!
—Hafiz

30

To Thine Own Self Be True
La Grande Class of '93 High School Graduation Address

June 1993

I feel honored to be here today and would like to thank everyone who made it possible: the Class of '93, parents, teachers, and especially Katie Kalemba. Thank you for this opportunity.

My mom, Rae Case, was born in 1914 in a log cabin in Range, Oregon, which I don't think exists anymore. She grew up on a cattle and horse ranch on Case Ridge, close to Dale. She went to school in Ukiah as a kid and then Weston. So even though I don't live here, I feel like I have roots in this part of the country. Her stories when I was growing up were filled with the majesty of the country and the realness of the people. I'd actually like to thank my mom today too. Her pioneer spirit and earthy pragmatism have helped me be here with you today.

We live in a world that is filled with paradox, that is very often beyond understanding. A world where grain silos are full in some countries, and yet in those same countries, people are starving…

starving not only for something to eat, but starving for respect and kindness too. A world where some children are pampered and given everything they could ever dream of, the love of their families, material possessions, and unlimited opportunities. Yet other children are deprived of the humblest affections and comforts and deprived of the simplest opportunities. A world where decisions are made in the name of business—like profit at any cost—decisions that are harmful to our planet, our health, our spiritual well-being, and our future. The kind of decisions that the very same person wouldn't even consider implementing in their private life.

The longer I live, and the more I investigate life, the more I realize that paradox has been with us for as long as there has been life. In a world full of paradox, where contradictory things exist at the same time, like good and evil, peace and war, love and hate, success and failure, abundance and poverty, a world of extremes, I have been pondering what words I can offer the class of 1993, to inspire you to live the richest life possible. And in twenty minutes too! I am used to teaching seminars that last several days, and that never feels like enough time. I hope that didn't get you worried!

What better place to start than with the motto the Class of 1993 has chosen for themselves?

"This above all, to thine own self be true."

Your chosen motto is a powerful and courageous credo to take with you when entering into this world of great paradox, especially when you know what your "truth" is and you have the strength and desire to "be" it. Most of us don't have a clue about how to be true to ourselves. That's why there are so many unhappy people!

Have you ever asked yourself the question, "Who am I?" and driven yourself a little crazy? In order to be true to yourself, there are some things you must "do first" to put your credo into practice. There are five essentials.

1. In order to know yourself and be true to yourself, you must have a very healthy relationship with the truth. Your truth and other people's truths too. You must want to know what the truth is! Most of us are afraid to know, so afraid that what we do won't be approved of by those we care about, or that

if we really be ourselves, we will be disapproved of, perhaps even lose those we care most about. When was the last time you asked someone you care about for feedback about something you did that didn't work, really wanting to hear their comments? If we aren't asking, that says we aren't open to the truth.

Our openness to embracing the truth is our greatest strength. Let me ask you two questions, "How much of your time do you spend editing your thoughts and what you are going to say next?" and "Why do you do it?"

We have all sorts of great reasons, the essential one is, we are afraid our truth will create consequences we don't want. By withholding our truth from ourselves and others, we create our own anonymity! When we learn to express our feelings, thoughts, and wants, we are free to discover and share our real self.

2. You must decide what kind of person you want to become, a vision or description of your ideal self. We live in a goal-oriented society, which is good. And yet most, if not all, the goals are about what we will do—education, work, family, financial status, etc.—and what we will have—house, car, clothing, health insurance. Very seldom do you hear a person declaring a goal to be honest, courageous, kind, adventuresome, or perhaps to live with integrity. The way our culture works is, you do what you can to have the things that you want so you can be the kind of person you want to be. Do, have, be. I would rather live in a culture where you be yourself and have the experience you want, so that you can do what is most important for you to do.

I love T-shirt art, and one of my favorites is

To do is to be —Socrates

To be is to do —Plato

Do be do be do —Sinatra

What kind of a person do you want to become?

3. You must determine what kind of a legacy you want to leave and how you want to be remembered. You may be saying to yourself, "Give me a break! I am just getting out of high school. How am I supposed to know how I want to be remembered? That's too far off!" Please listen…we live in a

society that is addicted to short-term gains, to new and improved, and we are suffering from it deeply. What is every addiction? A desire for a quick change of feeling or experience without any real investment on our part. It comes from a substance or behavior that over time will control us. If each of us took a longer-term approach, investing in our lives by thinking about what we want our lives to stand for, what we want to contribute and leave behind, we would see positive changes in our society fast.

4. In order to be true to yourself, you must do what is most important for you to do. You have got to take action! Do something, anything, that starts the ball rolling. It took me a long time to learn that the only life I could live was my own, and a lot of people were happy when I figured it out too. Nobody can do life for us. You are the only person you can change, and the results we create are through our own action, nobody else's. I wish someone had told me, simply and clearly, that I could build my self-respect and self-esteem by doing my very best, doing exactly what I said I would do, and acknowledging myself and others for our efforts.

How will you know if it is the most important thing for you to do? By listening to your heart, your inner voice, and by valuing your gifts and talents. Sometimes we make our lives very difficult by thinking that if it's not hard, it's not worthwhile. Our biggest gifts usually are easy for us. They may take work to master, but they feel natural. Please turn toward your gifts, not away.

5. To thine own self be true. You must accept that you are an important part of the human race, the human family. So often I hear people of all ages, sizes, and colors say, "There are so many of us, what difference do I make?"

It's because there are so many of us that it is vitally important that each of us knows that we are important and inside the human family. We are part of what makes up the "common good," the very structure and quality of our world.

This may sound strange and even comical, at the same time it was very painful. As a child, I thought I came from another planet! Oh yes, I thought I was so different that I had to be from another solar system! And how was I different? I knew deep in my heart when people weren't being kind or honest. With the eyes and innocence of our youth, I think we all knew that and then one day we said, "Why try to change it? That's just the way it is."

Yes, we are all different with unique talents and gifts, and at the same time, we are human. It's when we exclude ourselves that we start playing by rules that may be harmful to the whole. What if it is your truth your family is waiting for to be more whole? What if it is your truth your school is waiting for to be an even better school? What if it is your truth your town is waiting for to become an even better town? What if it is your truth the world is waiting for to become a better world? To thine own self be true does not mean exclusion, it means being your whole self while being part of what is going on! A whole self respecting and nurturing other whole selves.

With these five essentials as your guides, being true to yourself will be a natural and expansive process.

1. Having a very healthy relationship with the truth
2. Deciding what kind of person you want to become, a vision of your ideal self
3. Determining what kind of a legacy you want to leave and how you want to be remembered
4. Doing what is most important for you to do
5. Accepting that you are an important part of the human race, the human family

Are there setbacks in life? You bet—life is lumpy! How we deal with the lumps is a sign of our character, our best self. Life is glorious too. We have balance in our lives when we embrace both the highs and the lows, feeling our pain and our joy fully.

Class of 1993, here is my closing question to you, "Are you reaching for a TV remote, a computer game, your headphones, or are you reaching for the stars?"

Your family, town, country, and world are in need of you. We need you to be committed to being your true self and using your gifts and talents. It's time.

Reflections

1. Take a moment to reflect on your beliefs about telling the truth, the whole truth—especially the beliefs that stop you from telling the truth. Example: the truth hurts.

2. How much time do you spend editing your thoughts and what you are going to say next? What is the impact?

3. Evaluate yourself on the five essentials of being true to yourself and choose at least one new behavior for each that will strengthen your self-awareness.

Tender moments, Karen Claussen and Guido Bandioli

Half Empty, Half Full? Who Decides?

In the spiritual journey,
the compass unfailingly points
toward compassion.
Keep heading in the direction
that leads toward deepening your love
and care for all living beings,
including yourself.

—Paul Ferrini

31

Half Empty, Half Full? Who Decides?

September 1993

Have you ever noticed that there are so many theories about how the world works, from the flat earth view to circumnavigation of the globe, from Newtonian theory to Quantum physics and chaos theory? At one time these theories were fought, then questioned, and then with the passage of time accepted as scientific truth. You'll notice that our theories about how things work have changed. And yet one thing remains consistent in all these theories: they are based in relationship, how one thing relates to another.

Being aware of the larger scheme helps us notice similar patterns in our own daily life, how what's happening outside is happening inside ourselves. Take a moment to think about your daily life and notice if there is a time when you are not in relationship with something. When you look closely, you'll notice you are always in relationship to something or someone, and more importantly to yourself, though you may not be conscious of this relationship. The quality of each interaction either builds, lowers, or maintains your state of well-being and happiness.

What is it you long for in your relationships with the people you care about most? What's missing for you? How do you feel empty? Perhaps you long to know that you are loved unconditionally, respected not only for what you do but also for who you are, understood even in those moments of confusion, valued and important to the other, and perhaps something as basic as longing to know you are attractive. What do you want that you are not getting?

When what we long for is not there, and our expectations are not met by others, we experience pain. We usually think it is about the other person. They are not doing something for us, and we are not getting what we want from the outside. "They" are creating our feelings of hurt, loss, suffering, and powerlessness!

When you think of each of the things you long for, you will see they are mostly things you want from the outside, from others. As long as we are dependent on others for our fullness, we feel powerless, caught in an endless cycle of seeking approval, and the illusion that it is about the other person.

How to make the shift from half empty to half full, from scarcity to abundance?

When we stop and take ownership, we become aware that the quality of our experience is based solely on our interpretation of what's going on. Moment to moment, each of us is creating our own reality, our feelings, thoughts, and wants through our beliefs, assumptions, and interpretations of our world. Add in our fear of not getting what we want and we feel "half empty" or completely empty very quickly.

The first and most powerful step toward fullness is accepting that you are the source of your life experience—all of it. And this is the great news, because when I am the source of something, I can change it. If you are the source of my sadness, I have to wait for you to change before my life improves. Taking ownership is a step we take again and again because we have been taught to think that we are at the effect of others.

The second step is unconditional self-acceptance, appreciating all aspects of yourself instead of constantly judging. You know how to accept others, now it is your turn to accept yourself. Remember, a weakness is just a strength overused!

Wings' mission is to inspire and support positive change, creating an abundant, loving, and respectful world community. We are committed to providing you, your family, friends, co-workers, and anyone who will listen, with an inspiring and safe environment to enrich your life by noticing how you relate to what is already there, and opening to what is possible.

Imagine what it would be like if, where you are fearful in your relationships, you begin to trust yourself. This one change in your perception will transform your life.

Instead of half full, why not go for it all!

Reflections

1. What is it you long for in your relationships with the people you care about most? What's missing for you? How do you feel empty?

2. Who have you been most dependent on for acceptance and approval? What have you done in that relationship to get approval?

3. What have you wanted others to acknowledge and love about you?

4. What will it take for you to give yourself the approval you long for, to accept your own magnificence?

Wildflower *Osbeckia stellata*, Bhutan

Living Awake

I am happy even before I have a reason.

—Hafiz

32

Living Awake

October 1994

Have you noticed that when you live life focused on the many details of each day, you can lose your awareness of what's really going on? It's called busyness, hustling and bustling, getting things done, a sense of urgency and accomplishment, proving to ourselves and others that "I can do it!" As the details that make the most noise get our attention, others fall through the cracks, piling up and adding to our frustration. And then someone has the gall to want our personal attention. An interruption by your children or co-workers and you think, "How can they be so_____? Don't they know I'm busy?" Sound familiar? Stressful? Depressing?

Falling asleep at night thinking of what you haven't done and have yet to do is debilitating. We are caught like a rat in a maze, asleep at the wheel. One of my favorite quotes is, "The trouble with the rat race is even if you win, you are still a rat!" by Lily Tomlin. The rat race is actually encouraged in so many ways by our culture, we are even rewarded for it.

We have hundreds of interest groups wanting our attention, for us to think their way—the media, political groups, environmental groups, civic groups, religious groups, multinational corporations, the list goes on and on. We are inundated with other people's messages and values over and over again.

Sometimes we can feel so overstimulated with these often conflicting messages that we fall asleep, numb out. It's just too much to deal with. So we focus on the details of our own lives, because we have some control there, and we keep working away. Don't get me wrong, focusing on the details of our lives is extremely important and effective when the details are aligned with our deepest values. If they're not, we are just busy and in denial of our greatest strength—choice.

Living awake. What does it mean?

To me, it means being present in our lives, each day, each moment, in such a way that we are choosing consciously from our deepest values and intentions and then taking the appropriate actions to create what we want. Living awake is living in community with not only other people, but with all living things, accepting ourselves as part of the ecosystem, not "the" ecosystem. Living awake is realizing that there is not just one truth; each person's truth is a reflection of their belief system, and there is more that we don't know than what we do know. Living awake is joining each moment and exploring what is, instead of reacting to what we believe is there. Living awake is wanting to experience life fully.

What does it take? Two things: courage and attention. The courage to see clearly, to inquire, to truly listen, and to take action on your wisdom. The courage to honestly be yourself and show up in life, standing up for what you value. The courage to live in integrity, being authentic and whole, keeping your agreements. The courage to be vulnerable, to drop the masks we have designed to protect ourselves and to follow our hearts. The courage to live spontaneously, unattached to outcomes, trusting ourselves and life as the teacher. It takes commitment. It takes grit.

There are several sayings that remind me of the power of attention:

1. "What gets watered grows."

2. "What you focus on determines what you miss."

3. "What you give your attention to grows stronger."

If you don't have enough time for what's most important, it means you are giving your time to distractions and busyness, actions that give you a short-term sense of accomplishment and yet may totally take your attention away from what you value most.

Being present is a powerful and generative state of being—pausing and breathing, noticing what is most important. Maybe it's time to stop the grip of the clock and multitasking and start the power of conscious choice, presence, and focusing on what's most important.

How we live demonstrates what we really know. Living awake is remembering this and making adjustments when we don't like the story we are creating!

Reflections

1. When you honestly look at your everyday patterns of behavior and how much time you are giving to things each day, what do your actions say your priorities really are?

2. How do you feel about that?

3. What are your deepest values?

4. Make a list of what's most important to you and prioritize the list in such a way that you are living according to your deepest values, living awake.

Enchanted path to Tashigang Gompa, Bhutan

Life is not a journey to the grave
with the intention of arriving safely
in a pretty and well preserved body,
but rather to skid in broadside,
thoroughly used up, totally worn out,
and loudly proclaiming…
WOW! What a Ride!
—Mary Morrow Hagle

33

~~~

Crystal-Clear Vision, Better Than Twenty-Twenty

Lately, I am constantly walking around in a state called "goose bumps!" My skin feeling extra alive and sensitive to what's happening right now, my whole being in a state of just-right excitement, food tastes extra delicious, and all my senses are vibrantly turned on! Whatever I am involved in or working on is coming together with ease and amazing quality, and then leading naturally to my next involvement, which is right on track with where I want to go.

Once or twice, I've caught myself wondering if I'm missing something—like the hard part—and I realize I'm not used to such ease, so little resistance, anxiety, or concern about my next step. When I realize I am doing this, looking for the hard part, I stop, breathe, and then I relax. I let go of my imagined-worry memories and step right back into the flow state.

These feelings and the results I'm creating are too good to just let them be a blip on my radar screen of life. So I've been paying attention to how this all came about. I keep asking myself this question: "What am I doing differently to create this ease and these great results?" I stay open-minded, curious, listening to my own responses, and this is what I learned.

The recipe is simple. That is not to say it is easy. Taking the action is a little more involved. What am I doing differently? I let go of my fear of knowing my truth and what that could lead to. I let go of my expectations of how life is supposed to be. I let go of worrying about whether you will like me or not; I let go of my fear that "they" would laugh at me. I let go of thinking that I could never do enough, be enough, have enough. I let go of judging my own dreams. I let go of my past limitations and looked to my future. My future, my own creation!

And my vision became crystal clear. I found a place inside my heart, mind, and spirit so peaceful and yet exhilarating that I burst out laughing! I let myself see how I want my life to be at home in my relationships with my husband, sons, and family. I let myself see what I want to create in my work with my staff, participants, breast cancer survivors. I let myself see the impact I want to have wherever I am, and even where I am not, in this world crying out for inspiration. I let myself see how and where I want to invest my time and with whom, my community involvement, and most of all what I want Wings to stand for and to be. And I am simply doing those things. I chose them with every ounce of my being!

Like I said before, the recipe is easy; taking the action is where the work takes place, where the transformation occurs. Doing the action is where my fear of the unknown raises its scary head and tells me, "Don't do it. They will think you are weird! This is dangerous." However, when my vision is compelling, makes my heart go flip-flop in a great way, when I know it is what I really want, my passion pulls me through my fear. My courage helps me calm my anxious heart and do what I know will fulfill my dreams.

Will there be bumps and lumps along the way? Of course. Lumps are part of life, those unexpected events that are outside the story we have written for ourselves, that challenge us to rise up above our fears and be our best selves. Will my vision take me to places I can't see yet? Of course. Pioneers do not know for sure where they are going, and surprises are a delightful part of life. Will I be doing what I want to do, and spending time with people, like you, who I want to be with? Yes, because I am stepping into my vision again and again and living it with the support of so many loving and inspired people…fellow travelers.

Seeing our vision clearly and then choosing it again and again at each choice point is the key to freedom, fulfillment, and personal success. What do you want your life to stand for? How do you want to be remembered? Is it time to let yourself dream big?

May every day of your life be filled with joy, abundance, right action, truth, compassion, creativity, friends, and your crystal-clear vision to lead the way.

Reflections

1. What are you doing when you feel most alive, present, and fulfilled?

2. In the past, what have you thought that made doing things feel hard for you?

3. What have you been afraid others would think of you if you did what you wanted most?

4. If you knew you would be remembered for three things at the end of your life, what would you want them to be?

Taking off in Bhutan!

Dive In and Take Flight

When in doubt, make a fool of yourself.
There is a microscopically thin line
between being brilliantly creative
and acting like the most gigantic idiot on earth.
So what the hell, leap.

—Cynthia Heimel

34

Dive In and Take Flight

August 1995

Do you ever feel as if you were watching your own life go by? That your life isn't really about you, it's going on without you? You can see it happening "out there," and yet you aren't there? You do not feel emotionally engaged or really present in your relationships, your work, maybe even in your play time.

Many people reveal in the Personal Effectiveness Seminar that this feeling of disassociation is predominant in their lives. In this disassociated state, the major feeling is fear, which we don't like to experience. It's uncomfortable! So we shift it a bit and turn our fear into feelings of isolation, loneliness, lifelessness, unworthiness, despair, apathy, powerlessness, resentment, blame, depression (the national pastime), all our favorites. I don't think so!

Why do we watch, stand back from our own lives? Why do we settle for so much less than we really want? Again, all the old favorites based in fear: fear of rejection, fear of loss, fear of being laughed at, humiliated, shamed, fear that what we do won't be "right" or good enough, fear of being found out. If you look deeply at all these fears, you will notice they roll into one. If we get involved, in some way we will lose—fear of loss. And so we stand back, not speaking our whole truth of what we are feeling, thinking, and wanting, not risking by letting those around us know how much we care or how much we have to offer.

At what cost? A cost so extreme, so painful, a cost none of us can afford to pay. We lose ourselves. The very protection we created to keep us from the pain of loss creates the biggest loss of all.

Imagine for a moment that a large, deep, pristine pool of water has been part of your life since childhood. You've walked by it each day, sometimes quickly, sometimes lingering. You've observed it during all the seasons. You've sat beside it dreaming and wondering. You've seen the water clear blue, languid, shimmering, and inviting. You've seen it whipped by the wind, choppy and almost black, mysterious and threatening. You've splashed the refreshing water on your face and let your feet be cooled by the shallows, and yet you've never been in the pool. Do you know it? Have you accepted all that it has to offer you?

The difference between watching life go by and living it is diving in, getting all wet. Not just a toe or a finger, all of you.

The moment you dive in, there is nothing else to experience, just that moment and the moment to follow. In order to live, you must interact with the water, explore its depths, or float on the surface looking at the clouds go by. The more you involve yourself and play in the water, the more skilled you become and the stronger you feel.

You and the pool are one. The pool is the essence of you and the content of your life. So many of us say we want something different than what we have, and yet we don't know what we do have. By being fully engaged with your current reality, exploring your beliefs, behaviors, values, results, and accepting your ownership in creating it all, you have a powerful starting point to float on your back and watch the clouds go by as you envision what you want to create in your life and what you want to stand for.

The first step in taking flight, soaring free, and creating what you want most is to dive in and claim what is all yours right now. The exploration is the most important and rewarding one you will ever embark upon.

At Wings, we have excellent dive, swim, and flight instructors. Come on in, the water's fine!

Reflections

1. Do you ever feel that you are watching your own life go by, watching others get what they want? If yes, what are you settling for?

2. What are your biggest fears?

3. Instead of facing your fears, what do you do?

4. If you had no fears and were guaranteed success, what would you do?

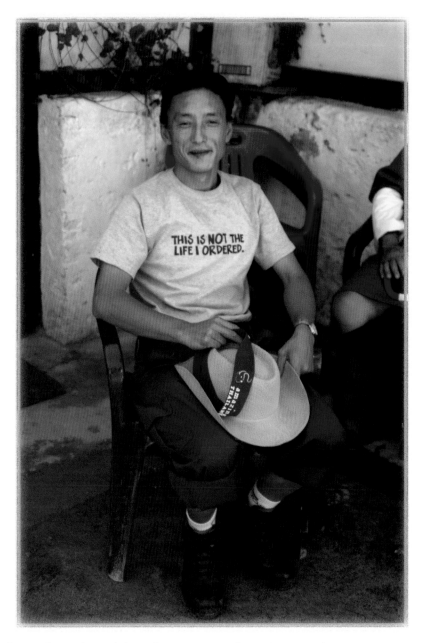

Check out the T-shirt of this Bhutanese guide resting at Taktsang Monastery café

What Was I Seeking?

I hear, I forget
I see, I remember
I do, I understand.
—Chinese Proverb

35

What Was I Seeking?
Reflections on the PES

January 1996

I am constantly amazed at the power of this work and what we create as a result. Imagine it's Sunday afternoon in the Seattle Personal Effectiveness Seminar. We've spent four days together learning and growing. Jim Klauser asks if he can read a poem he wrote the night before.

> What Was I Seeking?
> Reflections on the PES
> by Jim Klauser
>
> I came looking for something, I wasn't quite sure.
> Direction? Some guidance? A conscience made pure?
> Or maybe a chance to gain peace, or be free?
> Perhaps all of these—or how to just be.
>
> I thought I was open and knew what I had.
> My life was so full, and really not bad.
> But something was missing, I didn't know why,

So I came to the class—I'd give it a try.

But there was no TRY, only DO or NOT DO,
And beliefs that lie hidden, I'm aware of a few
That limit my options and give shape to my life;
Some lead me to action, others cause strife.

What I found was a choice for me now to own
The things that I've done, the past I condone,
And the things that I wish I could simply forget.
They're all part of me, all my doing and yet,

I'm much more than my past, the sum of my deeds
Or the times that I've scored, and grabbed what I need.
It's my being that counts, just the presence of one
That speaks to the world and can shine like the sun

When I take the time to just listen to you
Or look in your face and it's just between two
Where our spirits can touch and be close as doves
Open and free, expressing our love.

And what do I see when I look in your eyes?
Is it fear? or aliveness? some mask? or disguise?
No, I see a deep beauty, a child unconstrained.
We embrace and share closeness, for moments remain

In a state where time stops, only being that counts
And we find in this moment, our power it mounts.
This discovery, this birth, is what I had sought,
A chance to be touched and to share this one thought

That I can be the source of much grace
When I choose to be open and give others space
To reach out to me and share their true love.
It's a mutual mirror of grace from above.

It's LOVE and RESPECT that I'm called to exhibit.
Say good-bye to dependency, at SOURCE I will live it.
To live in intention, and master WIN/WIN,
Where no one must loose, or be put down again.

It's music I'm asked to play with my life,
Like twenty-two cellos cutting war like a knife.
And this song has a name that will set the world free.
It's clear and it's bright—it's INTEGRITY.

And it flows from my words, it's imbedded in truth,
To keep my commitments, a return to my youth
When yes meant yes, and no meant no,
And life was much simpler and I went with the flow.

Forgiveness was here, I found my soul's healing
To cleanse those in my past, and share a deep feeling
Of love and respect for all those I've known
And those that I've hurt, I claim as my own.

So what did I gain from this PES?
Was it just information? No, it was a YES
To my life and to all those I see.
What I got was a chance—to come home to ME!

I wrote this poem just before going to bed on the next-to-last day of my Personal Effectiveness Seminar. It's a gift to all those who participated in the PES conducted January 25–28, 1996, in Seattle—and to those who have worked to make this program a reality in mine and others' lives. Blessings.

—Jim Klauser

Jim, thank you for sharing yourself and the impact of the Personal Effectiveness Seminar with us all.

Reflections

1. Take a few minutes to relax and remember an experience in your life that was very meaningful for you. Bring the event clearly into your mind and write a poem about it. Let yourself use vibrant words to share your truth.

2. Bring to mind someone you would like to share your poem with and read it to them.

3. What did you learn about yourself by doing this assignment?

School boy at play, Bhutan

Hop, Skip, and a Jump!

Life is a great big canvas, and you should throw all the paint on it you can.

—Danny Kaye

36

Hop, Skip, and a Jump!

Even though there has been snow on the ground for the past few weeks, a true delight for me, something inside of me is whispering, "Spring!" Are there many clues that spring is on its way? Definitely not—not in this cold and slush. And yet, as I look at the stars, crystal clear in the night air, and I watch the stately magnolia out my window, I anticipate that spring is on its way.

Do you remember the anticipation you felt as a child before something "new" happened? Something that you had never experienced before, or maybe something that you knew you loved and it only happened once in a great while? Your anticipation, a delightful pressure building up inside, knowing that in a little while you would be a part of something beyond your knowing...wondrous. Perhaps it was like waiting for the beautiful curtain at our Hult Performing Arts Center to slowly open, revealing the magic and mystery of music and motion. Exquisite agony!

Do you remember when life was as easy as a hop, a skip, and a jump? When jumping right in the center of a puddle was the way to go, instead of carefully walking around it? Back when the secrets you had with your best friends were the essence of camaraderie and trust? Can you remember when you believed your world was a magical, mysterious place to explore and investigate with awe and delight?

Has that curious delight and anticipation been missing from your life for a while? It is amazing that over the years we seem to learn to back away from so much of what life has to offer. I know we have what we think at the time are "good reasons" for becoming very cautious. Isn't one of the mantras we hear our parents say in childhood, "Be careful!"?

We are taught that the world is unsafe or uncomfortable, and we have experiences that validate those beliefs. They become very real in our own experience. We start to spend our time figuring out how to avoid the pain and how to be comfortable. That's all well and good at the time; it kept us safe and out of trouble. The sad part is that as we grow and increase our ability to be resourceful in the world, we still operate as if we didn't have those resources and we keep being more careful than we need to be. We grow up thinking that is how "life" has to be, painting ourselves slowly into a drab corner, avoiding the pain.

Something I am realizing right now is how much pain we create for ourselves by avoiding the pain! I have stopped myself so many times in my life saying no to an action that just might, possibly, could, or perhaps sometime would under certain circumstances, hurt me. Sounds like a certain ticket to isolation and boredom!

Maybe it's time for us to look to the children so we can remember ourselves. Are you ready for something new in your life? Something like more fun and excitement, more meaning and inspiration? Could it be that it is as easy as "a hop, a skip, and a jump," right into the middle of...?

EXCITEMENT
Excitement is red.
It tastes like fresh baked cookies.
It sounds like people talking,

And it sounds like a forest.
Excitement looks like when somebody gets
an "A" on their paper.
It makes me feel like I'm ready for something.

—Christine Shevlin
Orchard Hill Elementary

1. Remember the anticipation you felt as a child before something "new" and good happened? Something that you had never experienced before, or maybe something that you knew you loved and it only happened once in a great while, like going to the circus? How would you describe this feeling of anticipation?

2. What were the events you looked forward to most as a kid? Were you alone or with others?

3. What do you want to look forward to now that will fill you with delicious anticipation? Go for it!

Mt. Jhomolhari, Bhutan

*The greatest discovery of my generation
is that a human being
can alter his life
by altering his attitudes of mind.*

—William James

37

Integrity, Service, and Vision

December 1996

"What makes Wings Seminars any different than all the other seminar companies? Why should I choose Wings?"

These are questions we often hear from people who have heard about the Personal Effectiveness Seminar and our training series over the twenty-plus years we have been in business. The people asking want more meaning and fulfillment in their lives and are curious about what we do and how we do it.

Provocative questions and rather ironic! Especially when one of the things we assist people to let go of in their lives is *comparison*! Rather than evaluating other companies and comparing ourselves to them, we choose to be very clear about who we are and what we specifically offer. From that foundation of information, we encourage each person to make a conscious choice, the best decision for them.

Dr. John Grinder, the co-founder of Neuro Linguistic Programming (NLP) and a dynamic teacher, was interviewed in July 1996 by Chris and Jules Collingwood of Inspiritive regarding teaching lasting life skills. He was asked, "What background skills and knowledge would you like to expect working NLP trainers to possess?" What follows is his response.

(In parentheses you will see the meaning I make of some NLP terms.)

He responded, "Personal congruity (integrity), sparkling intelligence, a deep, bottomless curiosity, a driving desire to discover new patterning, a phobic class response to repeating themselves (deep commitment to creating new insight and healthy behaviors), a continuous scanning for evidence that they are mistaken in every aspect of their personal and professional beliefs (thinking outside the box, open learners exploring life), solid personal ethics, physical fitness, actual real world experience in any field in which they intend to present NLP and an excellent sense of humor."

I think this is a powerful description of a masterful teacher and person. Each of our facilitators and staff members embody the qualities of which John Grinder spoke. I am honored to work with such talented and committed people!

What's equally important to me is that the company embodies these same qualities, that our vision is alive through each individual who works here. Wings' vision is to inspire and support positive change, creating an abundant, loving, and respectful world community. We practice corporate congruity, integrity, service, open learning, curiosity, commitment to excellence, and compassion. We practice what we teach.

Are we perfect? Do we always hit the mark? No, we are human and make mistakes just like everyone does. Yet our goal is to learn from our mistakes. We are committed learners who seek the highest good for all in each situation. Win-win is not just a concept for us, it is an ongoing practice.

Why am I telling you this? Because I believe you deserve the best, and what we offer is unique in its entirety. When you come to Wings Seminars or send someone, you will get the best we can create from the moment Claudia answers the phone, to the moment your seminar begins, to the moment you complete each seminar, and as long as you want to grow with us!

Do you have a clear vision of the life you want to live? Do you know your most compelling values? Do you know the legacy you want to leave behind? A meaningful life, one that is fulfilling for you every day, not just sometimes, is based in you knowing the answers to these questions and having the disciple to show up every day and live your answers.

Come learn powerful tools that will assist you to make healthy choices and decisions, that will keep your life focused, meaningful, and fabulous!

Reflections

1. What does integrity or congruity mean to you?

2. What are six of your greatest strengths? How do you demonstrate them?

3. What is the impact of your greatest strengths?

4. What is your vision for your life?

Tiger Swallowtail butterflies returning to my garden

Resurgence

Last night, as I was sleeping,
I dreamt—marvelous error!
that there was a fiery sun
here in my heart...
It was fiery because it gave warmth
as if from a hearth
and it was sun
because it gave light
and brought tears to my eyes.
—Antonio Machado

38

Resurgence

March 1997

The definition of resurgence is to rise again, a lifting up, a coming back to life.

As I look out my window, I not only see, I also hear and feel the subtle resurgence of the life cycle beginning again. *Spring*, slow as rising sap, is making its graceful way through all living things, buds taking form, grass brightening, the mating dance of birds and frogs croaking in our pond.

There have been times in my life when I thought that spring, a natural resurgence, was happening in every living thing except me, that in some way I was outside the normal cycle of life, dormant, cold, and lifeless. Those times were the most painful I have ever known: the last months of my chemotherapy when I realized that soon I would be on my own without drugs to fight my cancer, my longevity in question; the darkest and most disconnected years with my husband, Kyle; and the first few years of agonized grieving after my son Matthew's death. A part of me refused to be touched by the grace of new life and the renewal of spirit, and in my refusal I felt anguish, isolation, and anger.

Have you ever known such a time? Angry that others are flourishing while you languish, resentful that others can laugh when you feel such pain, envious of how easy it seems for others to get on with life, bitter that others have what you want and you don't know how to create it, and certain that you will always feel this way? Often these are the times that we don't want to recall, because the pain and suffering are so extreme.

As I refused to be nurtured by the natural cycles of healing and rebirth, holding on to my pain, I became organically aware of the deepest pain of all: denial of life and spirit, walking death. Here I was alive, but not living. How very egotistical of me to think I could control the very cycle of regeneration!

In its own time, gently, naturally, without fanfare or force, life seeped back again within me at a depth and breadth I had never known. It was as if a huge boulder had been lifted from my heart, mind, and spirit; colors were vibrant, music touched my soul, food tasted rich and luscious, and I heard the sound of my own laughter. How could such anguish lead to such joy and gratitude, such connection to life? I asked myself, "How I did I make the shift from suffering to peace?"

Instantly my answer filled me: surrender, yield, let go. In every instance of great suffering, the moment I let go of my expectations and "supposed to be's," my resurgence into life began. The moment I trust life, myself, and divine spirit enough to relinquish control over outside circumstances, I am free to discover my true nature. I am free to learn from events instead of fight, and I am free to experience life "now."

As I look back, I realize now that each of these times has been the seed bed of a dynamic resurgence in my life, my life enriched, transformed by what I learned from going with the cycle of life, not fighting it.

Through my breast cancer, I realized how grateful I am for my resilience, how committed I am to live and be healthy and strong in my mind, body, and spirit.

Reconstructing my relationship with my husband, Kyle, taught me the power of unconditional love, starting with myself, and that being passionately alive is inspiring. I also learned the power of accountably and respectfully telling the whole truth, all the time.

The death of my son Matt taught me to surrender, to let go of attachments to life being a certain way, and that thinking I can control events is a dangerous illusion. His death also taught me that there are no guarantees that I will be here for a long time, so to stop acting as if I had all the time in the world. Matt's death taught me to be fully alive *now* no matter what the circumstances!

1. What are the times in your life when you have felt distanced from life because of difficult events or experiences?

2. How did you take care of yourself through these times?

3. What did you learn from each event?

4. How are you using that learning to live fully right now?

Mark McInteer

Photo by Christopher Briscoe

December 27, 1945–August 3, 1997

To
mines
also de
Ha
slide, r
other,
vibrant
tions a
often a
On
McInte
spect, b
a thous
togethe
own po
Ma
people
geous,
An
love, ar
for who
Howev
ter, Abi
gift and

What lies before us
and what lies behind us
are small matters
compared to what lies within us.
And when we bring what is within
out into the world,
miracles happen.
                    —Henry David Thoreau

This one instance poignantly revealed to me *again* your true and indomitable character, wanting to give as much as you can give until the very last moment.

Your family, friends, and community hold you now in the circle of their arms and hearts tenderly, thankful that the circles of our lives have been blessed by your life, that your life has come full circle.

Thank you, dear friend, for sharing the miracle of life with me.

(Mark died shortly after this appeared in our newsletter and after returning from his trip to Disneyland with his family.)

Au

In

Oglal

be rou

wind,

ours.

form

person

"T

parad

and d

ut fro

us or

circle

1. Bring to mind someone you were naturally attracted to because of their true nature, and who touched your life in a positive way. Describe them and what you were attracted to.

2. What did you learn about yourself from this person?

3. Have you let this person know how important they are to you? If no, is now the time to acknowledge their contribution to your life?

Bhutanese children enjoying a special moment on a celebration holiday

Is It Time to Create the World You Want to Live In?

Care more
than others think wise.
Risk more
than others think safe.
Dream more
than others think practical.
Expect more
than others think possible.
— Howard Shultz, Chairman & CEO
Starbucks, Pour Your Heart into It

40

Is It Time to Create the World You Want to Live In?

November 1997

Now is always the best time to create the world you want to live in!

Every moment offers us the opportunity to either reveal our authentic self and who we want to become or to settle for what we think is expected, appropriate, or will keep us safely comfortable. Is it a risk to be authentic, to dream and stand for what we value as most important? Yes! And it is an even bigger risk *not* to because what we lose is our "self." We can create the world we want to live in, first within ourselves and then in our communications and interactions with others, when we know how. I firmly believe that people do what they know until they know better!

When I walk to the front of the room in the very first moments of the Personal Effectiveness Seminar, even before introducing myself, I ask the participants this question: "What kind of world do you want to live in? Not the material world of possessions and things. I mean, how do you want to feel moment to moment, and how would you ideally describe the quality of your relationships, personally and globally, if you could have them any way you want them?"

For a moment, I see a blank stare, which I interpret as, what the heck is she talking about? And then eagerly they begin to respond (I record their words on the board), the words pouring forth with candor and fervor. "The world I want to live in is safe, free, accountable, practices integrity, compassionate, full of laughter, generous, adventurous, a healthy community, respectful, loving, orderly, inspired, creative, powerful, connected, diverse, passionate, synergistic, kind, creative, thoughtful, peaceful, truthful, accepting, integrated, holistic, spiritual, abundant, wise, expansive, effective communication, unique, grateful, helpful, risk taking, responsive, and happy!" When the words stop and the board is full, I say, "I'm Kris King, and I'm here to assist you to create the world you just described. On Sunday we'll come back to this list and see if we've done it." Participants look both hopeful and skeptical.

Then for four days we delve into exploring consciousness and how it works. Together we learn new ways of thinking and seeing ourselves and the world that assist each person present to see themselves as the predominant creator in their lives, the actor on their own stage, not the acted upon. I have been doing this work since 1982, and I can honestly say I get to be present at the most miraculous moment in many people's lives, the moment they realize their own magnificence and that their lives are theirs to design. We practice many time-honored customs of being a healthy human being: accountability, forgiveness, and telling the whole truth respectfully. The list goes on and on. As the courage of each person is expressed and acknowledged, the group begins creating the world they want to live in!

Sunday afternoon, when I go back to the list, going over each descriptive word, both amazement and delight are clearly written on each face. When I ask, "Did we do it?" There is a resounding, "Yes!" and very often applause. Heartened by their awareness of our success individually and as a group, by their heightened sense of self-esteem and confidence in their new skills, each person makes their own personal commitment about going back into their lives and creating the world they want to live in *now*!

I believe the work of awakening to ownership, authenticity, compassion, aliveness, and service is what people are thirsty for and the lack of these qualities is what our culture is reeling from. Recently a rather humorous and far-reaching vision popped into my mind. I saw a world where Wings work, instead of being the exception, is the operating standard, as accepted, appreciated, and used as (get this!) toilet paper! You wouldn't think of operating in your daily life without it!

Imagine the impact that would have on the world. Well, in my vision, Wings is an exceptional brand with the very highest rate of customer satisfaction and use!

Are you ready? Changing the world one heart at a time is magic.

Reflections

1. Give yourself a few moments to envision the world you want to live in, how you want to feel moment to moment, and the qualities of your relationships, best-case scenario. Write it all down, no editing; just let it flow.

2. When you are done, take a moment to really see and feel the impact of these descriptive words, your choices. Describe the impact.

3. Is it time to have what you want? Are you ready to step more fully into your life? What will you do today to create the world you want to live in *now*?

Young monks walking to their monastery, Paro, Bhutan

What's Become of Honor?

Great ambition is the passion
of a great character.
Those endowed with it
may perform
very good or very bad acts.
All depends on the principles
which direct them.

—Napoleon Bonaparte

41

What's Become of Honor?

January 1998

Perhaps this is a time of evaluation for me. I have been looking back through the years of my life. Going back as far as I can remember and painting in pictures as clearly as memory will allow. It reminds me of turning pages in a very-much-loved old photo album. Memories of funny faces laughing, of first birthday parties, of grandparents with gentle faces who are no longer with me, of my piano recitals, of sports events, of the world news, of summer vacations, of school graduations, and of first love emerging, the story of my life unfolding. What I feel as I remember is a quickly changing kaleidoscope of emotions ranging from joy to sadness, from excitement to curiosity and gratitude. My precious life speaks to me.

As I look and remember, a realization is working its way into my conscious awareness. There were so many heroes in my life! People larger than life who taught me so many lessons. Not necessarily class content—although my seventh grade English teacher, Mr. Giordano, was amazing—the larger lessons about being a human being of honor. Each person taught me by their actions, by the way they lived each day, consistently displaying nobility of mind, action, and spirit.

If I were to write a list, it would be a long one, beginning with my parents, Rev. Bohm, Mrs. Wange, Dwight Eisenhower, President Truman, Eleanor Roosevelt, God, my brother Roger, my sister Carolyn, Martin Luther King Jr., Miss Wynn, my third grade teacher, JFK and on and on.

Heroes of time gone by became my heroes because they cared and did something about it. Each one my teacher, each one a whole person making mistakes along the way and correcting their course because they had a sense of honor, a reverence for life, and a deep desire to do the right thing. They wanted to make a contribution…right action.

Has something changed over the years? Are there still heroes in my life? Yes, and they seem to be fewer. Are there heroes in our children's lives? Yes, and I wonder what kind—especially when reading the newspaper or listening to the news. What kind of people do we as a whole hold up to our children as heroes, as people worth being our children's role models? How do we measure? Are our children finding their heroes these days in the sports pages, on TV, in church, in government, in show business, on YouTube—where? What values are we imbedding unconsciously into the minds of our young through the media?

What we value and acknowledge is all around us, and sometimes I feel ashamed. I see so much glitz and greed, addiction to power and drugs, notoriety, deception, looking good, and "me first" thinking. When we tell ourselves it's impossible to be a politician and be a person of honor, I think we are in trouble.

Who are your heroes, past and present? Is there a difference for you also?

Contrary to what you may be thinking, I am excited by my journey into my past and visiting my old heroes. Excited because with my new conscious awareness I can use what my old heroes taught me. It is time to acknowledge what I honor by choosing according to my deepest values: how I vote, who I invite into my life and my children's lives, how I run my business, how I spend the money I earn, who I support, how I invest my time, who I choose as my teachers. I want each choice to reflect what I hold precious.

Sometimes the simplest and quietest moments bring the greatest gifts and realizations. If I don't become a person of honor, who will?

Reflections

1. Looking back over your life as far back as you can remember, what are your fondest memories?

2. Who were your heroes as you were growing up? And why? What did they stand for?

3. Who are your heroes now? Is there a difference in what you are looking for?

4. What will it take on your part to think of yourself as a person of honor?

Dawn breaking in Bhutan

The Mandate Before Us

May all my life
be a mindful meditation.
May every action
be a prayer.
May I open
to divine
inspiration fully…
and be awake!

— Kris King

42

The Mandate Before Us

April 1998

When I wrote this piece ten years ago, I received the most feedback I had ever gotten on anything I wrote. It ranged from strongly positive—the best article to date, most courageous—to strongly negative—how arrogant and self-righteous I was to make such statements. As I am rereading it now, I realize I think we were at the same point then as we are now, and that is the learning. This mandate is right in front of us all the time, because we have been trained so well to be dependent on authority figures for guidance and approval. I am interested to know what you think. Here we go.

It is imperative that we mature—now. We've been waiting to be saved long enough.

Waiting through time to be saved from something ambiguous that we have called our sins, our enemies, loneliness, the government, disease, aging, drugs, poverty, the media, depression, the forces of nature, etc. Waiting to be saved from something ambiguous by something ambiguous, such as

God, the white knight, the perfect candidate, the perfect partner, the perfect career, the ultimate purchase, the perfect pill, vacation, or whatever. Waiting hasn't worked, and it will never work.

How much pain and suffering must you experience before you ask yourself, "Is there a better way?" How many nights and days of isolation, pain, and dissatisfaction can you stand? You see, our waiting to be saved is at the heart of the enduring, the waiting, the longing. Have you ever waited for a committed partner to change so you could be happy, all the while feeling resentment and anger, and blaming them for your feelings?

There is a mandate before us, now. To grow up, step into our own shoes, accept what we are and what we are capable of and be it. It is time.

I believe that we have spent the last century caught inside of two questions that have led us down a path of self-pity and disempowerment. These two questions are "Who am I ?" and "Why me?" Sigmund Freud gave birth to a huge industry that has helped people understand what could possibly be the answers to these questions. The reason I say, "could possibly" is, how can we possibly know in truth why things were the way they were in the past when we don't even know when it is happening in the present? We calm ourselves in the vast sea of ambiguity by making things up, creating stories that seem to make sense of why things are the way they are. The only reason for the ambiguity is that we have been asking the wrong questions.

The questions that we must ask ourselves now are "What am I?" and "What do I want my life to stand for?" instead of waiting to be saved by some outside forces. With these questions, we will save ourselves and be what we were meant to be, and in truth have always been.

Einstein said, "We can't solve problems by using the same kind of thinking we used when we created them." Until we choose higher consciousness and accountability, we will continue the patterns we have repeated for centuries.

Is what we have created in the past and the present, what you want to create in your future? If your answer is yes, read no further, and I wish you well.

If your answer is a clear no, come along. There's consciousness to raise, and it is yours and it is mine.

Reflections

1. Take a few moments to look back over your life asking yourself this question, "What have I been waiting for?"

2. What has been the impact on you of waiting for someone else to change so you could be happy?

3. What are your answers when you ask, "What am I, and what do I want my life to stand for?

4. What's one thing you will do right now to set that in motion?

Thai resting sculpture, Ko Samui

Divine Forgiveness

If we really want to love
we must learn how to forgive.

—Mother Teresa

43

Divine Forgiveness

October 1998

What is forgiveness?

At its essence, forgiveness means to *give as before*, before the breach you experienced with another, with yourself, to once again be connected with love, respect, and appreciation. The how of it—the hard part—is owning your own part and then giving up all claims against the other, a pardon, absolution, a letting go of all blame and resentments. Forgiveness takes away the barriers that you have built and maintained against yourself or between you and the other.

In *A Course in Miracles*, there is a statement that rocked my world when I read it for the first time. "Ask not to be forgiven, for this has already been accomplished. Ask, rather, to learn how to forgive." I thought, "What do you mean, it has already been accomplished? I'm hurt, I'm angry, and I know it's their fault!" Then I stopped and realized in Divinity's eyes there is no need for forgiveness because you and I are loved unconditionally. There is no holding against, only holding dear.

The heart of forgiveness is the unconditional love of God.

Why make amends, why forgive? Why is it so important? Making amends and forgiving are a letting go of victimhood. Any place you hold on to hurt, resentment, or anger, you hold your position as a victim. Attachment to blame, attachment to hurt, attachment to resentment—all are barriers to your personal freedom. Making amends and forgiving are ways of reclaiming your integrity. Where we have been or done things that are outside our value system, we have places where we blame ourselves, where we have relationships that are out of balance. We are out of balance.

Sometimes the intention of withholding forgiveness is to uphold some sense of self, of power, and yet over time the withholding causes a weakness because of our lack of integrity, of not being the kind of person you know you want to be.

Forgiveness is for the forgiver. When you will not forgive, you are saying, "I want to keep this wound," and you end up carrying people around inside of yourself like hostages, torturing yourself, holding yourself hostage too, creating a grotesque and profound separation from your own spiritual essence, your own heart.

It is vitally important to remember, forgiving is not a condoning of behavior nor a relinquishing of responsibility; it is an act of grace and accepting our humanness, that we make mistakes and our actions have an impact on ourselves and others.

Take a moment to breathe and come present, and then imagine yourself sitting in a big comfortable chair—a chair in which only truth is spoken or heard—and there before you is a big living screen, and one by one you begin to see the faces of the people you believe you have hurt. As you look into their eyes, you recall those moments of shock, pain, humiliation, disappointment, separation. Seeing the events, the people, noticing what you've done and thought and felt since that time, allow all your feelings to simply be there in your heart, noticing if they feel heavy.

Now the faces of the people on the screen begin to change to the people you believe have hurt you. One by one, you look in their eyes, remembering what they did or did not do that caused you pain, what has happened in each relationship since, the feelings you have carried for so long. As you watch, you realize how much energy you have given to each event, and you know it is time to release yourself and them, to let go, remembering the one who has probably hurt you the most is you. It is time to say, "I forgive you," feeling forgiveness filling your heart.

If your mind interrupts, saying they don't deserve to be forgiven, remember that forgiveness comes from the inside. No on can make you forgive. You are at choice about how free and loving you want to feel. Do not forgive anyone you are not ready to forgive, and be open to that changing as you open to power of making amends and divine forgiveness.

Reflections

1. Who do you believe you have hurt? What did you do or not do that caused them harm?

2. Who do you believe has hurt you? What did they do or not do that caused you harm?

3. What has been the impact on your relationships of holding on to past grievances and resentments against others and yourself?

4. Are you ready to be free again, to take ownership of your own life and forgive? If your answer is yes, congratulations. If it is no, what is it going to take?

Japanese iris in my garden

If we listened to our intellect,
we'd never have a love affair.
We'd never have a friendship.
We'd never go into business
because we'd be cynical.
Well, that's nonsense!
You've got to jump off cliffs
all the time
and build your wings
on the way down.

—Ray Bradbury

44

Reflections

April 1999

Having just returned from trekking in Solu Khumbu, Nepal, for the fourth time, relaxing on the beach in Thailand, and visiting my niece, Kristin, in Kyoto, Japan, I am spilling over with joyful experiences and vibrant memories that fill my heart with gratitude. So much happened during the thirty-seven days that I was in Asia that, in order to be conscious of what I learned, I've been spending time in silent reflection (my 600-plus photos as my guide). And I would like to share these reflections with you, my dear friends.

First: True riches and wealth lie in the heart of the experiencer, not in outside circumstances.

Nepal is ranked as one of the poorest nations in the world economically, and many would say, "Isn't that too bad." And yet, the Nepali are the some of the happiest and wealthiest people I have ever known. They are rich in love, relationships, and family; rich in healthy, nutritious food; rich in their connection to the earth, seasons, and the glorious Himalayas; rich in their spiritual beliefs, meaningful practices, and colorful rituals. Imagine this: in Kathmandu and throughout the country, Hindus and Buddhists actually share many holy shrines on a daily basis. Abundance is a personal experience.

Second: With positive intention, any activity can be a multifaceted blessing.

My intentions on this trek were to respectfully learn about Nepal and for the group to be positive representatives of our culture with everyone we encountered. As the fourteen of us bonded and became friends, trekked, learned Nepali, ate glorious, healthy food, had our vacations, and strengthened our bodies, the people who were in service to us also benefited deeply. To name just a few, our support staff, being experts about all things Nepali, practiced and learned English and about our culture. We created relationships with each other that will last a lifetime and opened our hearts and minds to embracing differences instead of fearing them. As a group, we chose to help Rumjatar Secondary School, impoverished and bursting at the seams, become a school where students have what they need to learn by building a library, and we also assisted with the reconstruction of the Lura monastery. Brains, hearts, and bodies all working together with positive intention are so powerful!

Third: "Don't you think laughter is prayer?" (Mary Greenwood).

Talk about happy! From Nepal, one of the poorest nations, to Thailand, an emerging nation, to Japan, one of the wealthiest nations in the world, there is a common thread of laughter, taking oneself and others lightly with grace and humor.

I have my ideas why this is so, one being that Buddhism is a prevalent practice in these three countries. When they pray, they are praying for the well-being of all, not just themselves. Imagine having your laughter be not only a joyful experience for you but an offering of grace and light to others as well! The second is that in all three countries there is a strong belief that healthy community is built by each individual fulfilling their part, that we have an impact on each other and it's each person's duty to be respectful of others.

Fourth: The smallest gift given with great love is more valuable than one that is given as a "have to."

So many times on the trail, we stopped and talked with a farmer tending his field, laughed with the children at our terrible pronunciation of Nepali words, said "Namasté!" to whoever passed by. In the past, I thought of gifts as physical things that I made or bought, and I always wanted them to be perfect. In Nepal, I realized that being fully present in the moment is a great gift to me and to whomever I am with. Ease, generosity, rapport, listening, laughter, and sometimes tears too. How precious to share them.

Fifth: Do it now. Life is too short to spend it sitting on the couch!

What are your dreams and desires? What gets your heart rate up, just by thinking about it? What are you longing to do that you have told yourself is too expensive, takes too much time, is too risky, etc.? These are the excuses we live with rather than having the lives we want.

Life is waiting for you to come to it. It doesn't work the other way! Jump in.

There is so much more, and my reflection continues.

Reflections

1. What does this mean to you? "True riches and wealth lie in the heart of the experiencer, not in outside circumstances."

2. What does this mean to you? "The smallest gift given with great love is more valuable than one that is given as a 'have to.'"

3. What are some of the most memorable "precious moments" in your life?

4. Who in your life do you want to spend more real time with, feeling connected and present? Will you initiate it?

My dad, Arnold Anderson, in flight school, 1942

A Life Without Regrets

Life is no brief candle to me.
It is a sort of splendid torch
which I have got a hold of for the moment,
and I want to make it burn
as brightly as possible
before handing it on to future generations.
　　　　　　　—George Bernard Shaw

45

A Life Without Regrets

November 2001

These last months since September 11, 2001, have been a riveting time personally, nationally, and globally. A time of reflection, remembering what is most important, and taking action. The possibility of a great awakening is at hand. What are the most important changes you want to make in your life so that you live a life without regrets?

Very often, when people awaken and grow, we get very excited about the future and the possibilities of what can happen. And very often, when people awaken and grow, we turn around, look at our past, and make it wrong, thinking that we should have somehow known "it" all along. We blame ourselves harshly for not growing sooner, and even worse, we may start blaming others—partners, friends, parents, the culture, you name it—for what happened in our past.

Actualizing ourselves to our highest and best selves, growing, is an ancient and well-recorded desire for humankind throughout history. There have been innumerable voices in every culture calling brothers and sisters to awaken to our goodness, to take peaceful and thoughtful action, to serve humankind, to make the world a joyous, safe, and compassionate place, and to reverently take care of the earth. Sometimes we listen, become inspired, and change. Sometimes we gradually stop, and like falling asleep, we don't realize when it happens.

Remember the first Earth Day? Did Earth Day awaken a part of you that deeply cares for our earth? Did you get really excited about the possibility of everyone pulling together to recycle and create great change? Have you judged people and cultures that aren't doing it the "right way"? Remember September 11, 2001? Are you still as aware of what's most important to you, or have you started to fall back into old habits?

If we make our past wrong when we experience insight and growth, or if, when the natural process of falling asleep occurs, we judge ourselves as wrong, our faith in ourselves erodes slowly and surely. To live a life without regrets, we must stay committed to valuing our past, our heritage. It has taken all of our past to create this moment and what comes next—every hurt, every tear, and every bit of laughter and love. When we don't listen to and honor our past experiences, we simply recreate them over and over again, blocking the road to our future.

There have been many awakening moments in my life: breast cancer, recreating my marriage to Kyle, starting Wings, the death of my son Matthew, September 11, and most recently the death of my father, Arnold T. Anderson. We celebrated his life on November 3, 2001. One of my great realizations while I was there with my mom and family was that I participated in my dad's life the best way I knew and I have only sweet and poignant memories, no regrets.

All of your life and mine is essential and priceless. To stay fully committed, we must value all of it. When you awaken and see life anew, no matter what the occasion or what it took to wake you up, savor the learning, celebrate, and do it, be it, say it now! Live a life without regrets.

This is what I wrote for my dad's memorial service:

I am forever blessed that Arnold T. Anderson is my father. A true father, unconditionally loving mentor, teacher, guiding light, guardian, and friend—Dad was all of these things and more to me, to my brother, Roger, and sister, Carolyn.

My dad was often shy, never calling attention to himself, a man of dignity and honor. People sought him out, relaxing in the full acceptance and attention he gave to everyone.

My dad laughed easily and never at anyone's expense.

He delighted in the unexpected and the curious, seeking to understand what life offered him—cultures of the world, how any "thing" worked, where the fish were, the perfect move in a dance step, the subtle hint of an herb in a sauce—all as he lovingly watched over his family.

My dad listened with the eagerness and curiosity of a child, seeking the truth instead of the easy or expected answer. Dad was both a teacher and a learner.

My dad believed that we are here to fulfill our heart's deepest longings, to do the best we can do in every moment and be happy doing it. And by his example, we learned this lesson.

My dad held his word as his bond. He simplified his life by only doing what was most important to him. He was a simple man of great depth.

My dad loved to create, to use his imagination in every aspect of his life: paintings, systems, cooking, designing their homes, singing—what a voice!

My dad loved my mom. By watching them together, from my earliest years until these last several years, I learned what true love means—unconditional and real, passionate, ever present, patient, and kind. Mom's courageous caring for dad was a reflection of the love they shared.

I want to share a view expressed by Bert Hellinger in his book *Acknowledging What Is*:

> I belong to life, or to a force that brings me into life and holds me, and then lets me drop out again. This way of seeing things seems to me to be much closer to the reality. One who experiences himself or herself as part of a greater whole experiences a supportive energy, although it's an energy that can also bring suffering. It's not our happiness that makes the world go round. It's something quite different; it calls us into its service and we have to yield to it. At the end of our time, we drop out of life back into something we know nothing about.
>
> We don't just suddenly appear out of nowhere. The life we receive through our parents is embedded in something greater. Something flows together in our parents and passes life on to us. We are already present in some sense, or we couldn't become. When we die, we're not gone, although we're not visible to the living any longer. But vanish? How can we vanish?
>
> Being, the depth behind everything, is beyond life. Compared with being, life is small and temporary.

I am grateful to you, Dad, for sharing life with me. Yes, Dad, you are dead…and I miss you. We will live a bit longer, and then we will come too.

Namasté.

Reflections

1. Describe several times in your life when you "woke up" and became excited about setting a new course of action.

2. Name the insights you are still excited about and why.

3. Name the insights to which you have "fallen asleep" and the impact on your life.

4. Now what are the most important changes you want to make in your life so that you live a life without regrets?

David and Alan Larson

Becoming an Exceptional Parent, Person

Alone we can do so little;
together we can do so much.
—Helen Keller

46

Becoming an Exceptional Parent, Person

July 2002

"Discovering the ways in which you are exceptional, the particular path you are meant to follow, is your business on this earth," said Bernie Siegel, MD, a pioneer in supporting cancer patients to change their perception of themselves from being a victim of cancer and disease to being an exceptional and courageous patient. I strongly agree with Dr. Siegel. I believe it is our task to accept and explore our own unique talents and gifts, to live our lives becoming more truly our best selves each day now—not waiting for a catastrophe to wake us up.

And yet so much of what happens in our lives has nothing to do with these discoveries. Much of what we are taught in life is devoted to directing, restraining, and containing us to fit a certain pattern that is called "culturally acceptable" and approved of by others. Am I saying that learning to follow the rules isn't important? No. I think some rules are vitally important to our health, welfare, and to our community.

What I am saying is that through our acculturation and learning process, sometimes the uniqueness, the spunk, the creativity, and the dignity of the individual are sacrificed. The intentions are good—to create structure, predictability, and safety. The results are not always so good—individuals feeling controlled and dependent upon authority figures, bored, and fearful of being judged, of making mistakes, and not belonging.

I believe we must live and behave in such a way that our children (our own and those we have a responsibility to) learn to appreciate their own magnificence and learn to take action for themselves that repeatedly reaffirms their accountability, magnificence, and capabilities. That sounds like a tall order when faced with an irate teenager! And how do we do this if we have not learned this ourselves?

To become an exceptional parent (person), or to assist others in becoming exceptional people, we must decide that discovering our uniqueness is valuable, possible, and worthy of our time and energy—because it will take time and energy! From there on it is a matter of learning ways that work and using them every day with ourselves and in our interactions with everyone, especially our children.

The ways that work are simple things, simple actions that show how much you care and what you stand for. Simple things like taking ownership of your own behavior rather than blaming others, receptive listening rather than judging and rebuttal, telling the whole truth instead of editing or lying, respecting rather than disregarding, unconditional loving rather than expecting, creating clear agreements and keeping them rather than forgetting, encouraging rather than controlling, and celebrating rather than criticizing.

Simple to understand, perhaps not so simple to apply, especially in those moments when you feel most challenged. However, isn't it amazing we want our teens to practice self-control when we are not? Imagine in those moments of feeling most challenged that you stop, breathe, and take ownership of your own behavior.

For example, "I just noticed that I am speaking loudly and using critical language as I am talking to you. I apologize. I think it is something I do with you when things don't go the way I want them to. I think I am afraid of conflict and don't know how to handle it very well. I feel sad and concerned that I do this with you. What I want is to understand you and for you to understand me. I want to really hear what you are saying. I want to make clear agreements with you that we both keep to build trust between us. How do you feel about what I just said?" And then really listen.

This may sound like a mouthful to you, and I want you to know that with practice you will transform not only the way you communicate, but the level of trust, clarity, love, and cooperation between you.

Why wait to be sick or to have a life-changing event come along before you accept and appreciate that you and your teen (partner, co-worker, etc.) are truly exceptional people? Use the actions listed above with yourself and your teen for a few days, or a lifetime, and you will be amazed at what you discover about yourself and your teen.

Reflections

1. When you were a kid, what do you think was the main focus of your parents' parenting? Teaching you through correcting, or celebrating your uniqueness?

2. What was the impact on you? What did you decide about taking risks?

3. Setting aside your self-judgment and being honest with yourself, how are you exceptional? What are your gifts and talents?

4. What do you want to start celebrating about yourself and others?

Tashi delek: good luck greeting from Bhutanese man

Doing the Right Thing: Miracles

Let yourself
be silently drawn
by the stronger pull
of what you really love.

— Rumi

47

Doing the Right Thing: Miracles

June 2003

One of the most valuable outcomes of conscious awareness, I believe, is the skill of healthy self-evaluation—knowing how to stand above the details and events of our lives and look down with curiosity, accountability, and objectivity to see what's working and what we want to do differently.

Some people think that self-evaluation is what goes on in their heads all the time, which for the most part is judgmental of self and others. This stream of criticism, when run to the extreme, is destructive and actually stops us from taking effective action. That is not self evaluation; it's "mind chatter"!

Gandhi said:

It's the action,

not the fruit of the action,

that's important.

You have to do the right thing.

It may not be in your power,

may not be in your time,

that there will be any fruit.

But that doesn't mean you stop doing the right thing.

You may never know what results

come from your action.

But if you do nothing, there will be no result.

Have you ever wondered what the "right thing" is? I've seen people freeze at the idea, stop dead in their tracks, fearing they could make a mistake, as if there is only one right thing to do! Knowing what the right thing is becomes apparent when we know our deepest values, our vision for our lives, practice healthy self-evaluation, and then take action. Action leads to learning, which helps us decide what the next right thing to do is.

When I participated in the Personal Effectiveness Seminar in 1982 at thirty-nine, I realized that most of my thoughts were based in faultfinding, and I was constantly comparing myself to others, sometimes one up, but mostly one down. No wonder I didn't know what I wanted in my life. I wasn't really focused on what I wanted; I was focused on getting away from what I didn't want! With the help of the teachings at Wings, I began the lifelong process of knowing what is the right thing for me to be, to do, and to have.

May 9, 2003, I turned sixty, and I am so delighted to be sixty! Since I had breast cancer at thirty-six, every year is a gift and a bonus. What a perfect time to self-evaluate.

Standing up above my life and looking down, I see what in 1982 I would have considered miracles because I thought my life was over.

I see and acknowledge

- ❧ my healthy and resilient body;
- ❧ my healthy and loving relationship with my husband, Kyle;
- ❧ my rich and delightful relationships with my sons, Mark and Kyle;
- ❧ running a business I love with people I respect and cherish;
- ❧ renovating a building so Wings has a beautiful home;
- ❧ supporting my mom and dad through his dementia and death;
- ❧ my vast friendships, teaching, and interacting with so many great people;
- ❧ my travels around the United States, to Tokyo, Nepal, Sweden and Bhutan;
- ❧ my ability to communicate my truth clearly with love and respect;
- ❧ all the beauty that surrounds me;
- ❧ the positive impact Wings has had on thousands of people's lives;
- ❧ all the fun I have had doing it all;
- ❧ and there's so much more!

I didn't know any of the above would work out. I just knew they were things that I wanted and were "the right things" for me to do. What do you want to look down and see when you look at your life?

It's always time to do the right thing. Ready for some miracles?

Reflections

1. Imagine standing up above your life and looking down at it. What do you want to see?

2. Why are these things important to you?

3. What are you doing right now to bring these things into reality?

4. How will you feel when what you want to see is your reality?

Bhutanese children sharing an open door and open hearts

What If?...Through the Eyes of Fear and Love

*Where service and vision meet,
creation accelerates
into miracles.*

— Kris King

48

What If?...Through the Eyes of Fear and Love

December 2004

"What if?" is a very powerful question because it invites us to be creative and envision the future.

However, I have noticed that very often this question is used in a fearful way. For example:

"What if I get sick?"

"What if they leave me?"

"What if I lose my job?"

"What if I never figure it (life) out?"

"What if the terrorists attack?"

"What if the sky falls?" (Henny Penny)

"What if I make a mistake about something important?"

The list goes on and on. Just notice how you felt reading these questions. Perhaps a loss of energy, concerned, fearful? Notice the images in your mind, perhaps remembering past inadequacies or hurts. The above questions set your imagination in motion with a negative focus, and the result is what I call "disaster films" with your life as the story line. Every time you imagine in this way, you imbed the fearful beliefs more strongly not only in your mind but also in your body. The result is often inaction and the feeling of being stuck, hopeless. Have you ever noticed this?

Imagine the shift in your results if you ask "what if" questions from a different perspective—the perspective of love.

"What if I take really good care of myself physically?"

"What if I love myself and others wholeheartedly?"

"What if I show up fully, using my skills and talents in life and in my work?"

"What if life offers me opportunities to learn every day?"

"What if my body is worthy of my loving care?"

"What if peace starts with me?"

"What if the universe really is a safe place?"

"What if taking a stand for something I believe in is exhilarating?"

"What if I can really have what I want?"

Again, notice how you felt as you read these questions. Perhaps curious, inspired, relaxed? Notice the images that came to mind. Times of your greatest resourcefulness and involvement? This use of "what if" invokes your imagination and creativity in a positive and enlivening way, of possibilities, dreams, and action.

By shifting our perspective from fear to love, we impact every aspect of our lives.

Have you been waiting in any part of your life, fearful that it won't turn out right? The quality of the questions we ask ourselves determines the quality of our lives. Is it time to start asking questions that reveal your desired present and future?

Every time you choose love over fear, you change the world and make it a better place for you and the people around you.

Wings is here to support you in daring to dream big and advocating for the world you want to live in.

Reflections

1. How have you used "what if" questions in the past?

2. What has been the impact on your thinking and how you feel about your life?

3. Make your own list of "what if" questions that are positive and open your mind to the possibilities of your life.

4. Notice how you feel when you read your list. Is it time to step into your desired future?

Lovely rice seller on market day in Bhutan

We've been waiting for you.
You are the only one
who can fulfill your part.
                    —Sue Miller Hurst

49

Envy vs. Emulate

July 2007

Envy

Pronunciation: 'en-vE

Definition: A feeling of discontent or covetousness with regard to another's advantages, success, or possessions (*Random House Dictionary of the English Language*, 2nd edition); a resentful awareness of an advantage enjoyed by another joined with a desire to possess the same advantage (*Merriam-Webster's Collegiate Dictionary*, 10th edition).

Late in the sixth century, Pope Gregory the Great made envy one of the seven deadly sins, which are defined as "deliberate violations of the will of God, a misuse of our free will and a deliberate turning away from God. Sin is a grave matter committed in full knowledge with full consent of the will; until it is repented it cuts the sinner off from God's sanctifying grace" (*Encyclopedia Britannica*, 200th anniversary edition).

What is it about envy that Christendom has seen it for centuries as a deliberate sin? The effect of deliberate sin is that we are cut off from God's grace, disconnected from our wholeness. We are out of balance in a profound way and feel it not only in our hearts and minds, but also in our bodies. The feeling is toxic. We experience hell right now.

Have you ever envied and resented someone who was really excellent at something? For being intelligent, talented, capable, beautiful, handsome, funny, athletic, doing what they love, fulfilled spiritually, charismatic, at ease socially, etc.? Where do you feel it in your body? What kinds of thoughts did you have about them?

Have you ever resented someone who had something you didn't have and thought you deserved? For example, healthy relationships, close friends, a great job, a lovely home, a car, a great wardrobe, a trip somewhere, money, a great body, etc.? What have you said inside your mind when you thought about this person? What have you said to others about this person behind their back? What do you feel in your body?

Our definition of resentment at Wings goes like this: "Resentment is like swallowing poison and expecting the other person to die." This is the feeling of envy. It gnaws at your mind, heart, and gut. And when you are feeling it, you may do or think things that you are not too proud of later, which means a double dose of guilt. Envy seems, in a way, to be safe, and it keeps us justified in not taking action of our own. However, envy is anything but safe. It is insidious and keeps us stuck in resentment, jealousy, longing, and "poor me" or victim thinking. Toxic.

When we envy another, we build separation between ourselves and them and also distance ourselves from the very things we want. They belong to the other, not to us.

Let's look at another possibility.

Emulate

Pronunciation: 'em-yU"lAt

Definition: A desire and effort to equal or excel, to imitate or model another's desired traits, capabilities, or possessions.

My mom gave me a great gift as I was growing up. She used to say to me, "If a human being can do it or create it, so can you." So I grew up believing that if I did my part, I could do just about anything (except be a man, which for a while I thought would be pretty cool). I watched people I admired and "tried them on," the way they walked, talked, painted, sang, played field hockey, danced, anything. I didn't realize I was emulating them or modeling them. I just watched very closely and then did what they did, and I learned. I went beyond my own frame of capability.

I am not saying that I never felt envy. Sometimes it was bitter in my mouth with words I wanted to say to diminish someone's brightness. Sometimes I felt so jealous of another's beauty that I couldn't sleep, feeling such angst in my body I thought I would die.

I am saying I found a way through envy to valuing, honoring, and appreciating others' talents, capabilities, and possessions, so that I could learn from them how to bring all that abundance into my own life. I began to emulate those I admired and blessed them for showing me the way. Who do you respect enough that you want to model them and grow?

Reflections

1. What role has envy played in your life?

2. Who have you envied? What capabilities of theirs did you envy? What impact did that have on you?

3. What possessions have you envied? What impact did that have on you?

4. Who do you want to emulate, to model their gifts and talents and make them your own?

Trekking friends David Larson and Sonam, Bhutan

Mastery...A Life Path

Each friend represents a world in us,
a world possibly not born
until they arrive,
and it is only by this meeting
that a new world is born.

—Anáis Nin

50

Mastery...A Life Path

October 2006

Master (edited from *Random House Dictionary of the English Language*, 2nd edition)

1. a person eminently skilled in something, as an occupation, art, or science 2. a person with the ability or power to use, control, or dispose of something. Syn. adept, expert, skillful, supreme, matchless, consummate.

Oh my, what a year this has been! A year filled with newness, of moving out of a place we had been in for five years and into our new location, of new staff with fresh ideas, and of some great new ways to fulfill our vision: to inspire and support positive change, creating an abundant, loving, and respectful world community.

As I look back at this year with deep gratitude for all the support of my staff, our wonderful participants, backup team members, and all the people involved with the renovation of this delightful space, I am amazed at the dedication and different types of mastery that brought it all together.

When I look even farther back in time, I realize that I had two of the best teachers in the whole world demonstrating mastery to me from the earliest I can remember: my mom and my dad. There is no way to tell you the hundreds of ways they showed me that bringing my whole self to whatever I did would not only serve me, but would serve the whole family and from there my community.

I am not talking about meeting expectations of perfection to please somebody else. I am talking about what I believe are the four keys to mastery.

- Expressing my passion for anything the best way I can
- Being an avid learner in that process
- Committing to deepening my skills through practice
- Sharing my capabilities in service to my world

I remember my dad teaching me how to make a mosaic for my eighth grade art class. He worked with me every step of the way, and yet I did all the work. He was patient and encouraging even when I messed up. He would chuckle and ask, "What did you just learn by doing it that way?"

My dad had a great laugh; remembering it fills my heart with joy and brings tears to my eyes, I miss him so. He had a keen eye for design, color, and use of space. His questions provoked me and challenged me. Through his drawings he helped me see the world in a whole new way. Wanting to please my dad, I worked very hard and held my breath for long periods of time. When he heard me exhale—whoosh!—he'd look at me and encourage me to relax into the creative process.

My mom showed me every single day about touching life with reverence, love, and humor from how she tended her gloxinias, prepared a meal, prepared to teach, raised corgis, washed the car, or played the piano. Her range of mastery was and still is incredible to me, and none of it was a push or a proving. It was all fueled by the love of what she chose into her life. My mom is the most fulfilled ninety-two-year-old I have ever known!

As I read what I have just written, I realize that these keys to mastery—expressing your passion for anything the best way you can, being an avid learner in that process, committing to deepening your skills through practice, and sharing your capabilities in service to your world—are what Wings is all about. I am so grateful that I can pass on what was given to me with such love.

Reflections

1. What are you passionate about?

2. Are you ready to express it? To commit fully and master it?

3. What will you risk to do it?

4. What will you risk if you do not do it?

My sons, Kyle and Mark, with my mom, Rae, at her last Christmas

She flies
with her own wings.
—Oregon state motto

51

The Call of Profound Integrity

June 2007

Personal Integrity: my principles, values, and actions are aligned. I keep my word with myself and others, telling the whole truth accountably without blame or judgment.

Profound Integrity: I hold my well-being as my responsibility, and I take care of myself physically, mentally, emotionally, and spiritually, and I am in service first to my family, myself, and my committed relationships (Wings definitions).

These words, "the call of profound integrity," have been running through my mind for weeks now—when looking out the window at spring unfolding, driving my car feeling the fresh air on my face, and moments when I am alone and aware of my connection to the divine. When I hear these words, I feel a sense of longing so intense that at times it takes my breath away, clutches my heart, and leaves me breathless. Integrity means wholeness, and part of me feels shattered.

My mother is dying. My longest loving relationship is coming to an end. This will happen only once in my lifetime, and I want to be there for my mom the best way I can while taking care of myself and my family too. Not a balancing act; rather, an authentic balancing of love, respect, and service that is nurturing and healing for all of us.

Sitting with my mom while she lies in bed, my brother, sister, and I tell stories of growing up together. We laugh, we cry, and mom listens and adds in. Then she is talking about her own growing up on the E Quarter Circle Ranch in eastern Oregon, remembering a laundry day when a chipmunk fell in a pot of apple butter and then ran through all the clean, folded sheets. We laugh, thinking of all those little footprints. She sighs, remembering how hard it was to do laundry then, how hard they all worked. Good memories, sad ones too. Ones you can't help having in a life ninety-three years long.

As we talk and I listen, I feel such a deep sense of gratitude for our time together…all of it. And in that moment, I realize how much my learning at Wings over the years is helping me be the person I want to be in this time of accepting a heartbreaking reality. I am eager to communicate what's in my heart instead of fearful, open to the changes I see in her instead of denying, standing up for what I think she wants instead of hoping some one else will, letting my tears be seen rather than hiding them, and so much more.

If someone told me I could teach only four things for the rest of my life, I know what I would choose: accountability, integrity, love, and service (vision). These are the things I most want to practice and that my mother demonstrated to me and everyone who knew her every day of her life. They are the foundations of a meaningful life.

My mom died peacefully on May 11 at about 5:00 a.m., a gentle smile on her face. The days leading up to her death are some of the most poignant of my life. I am so thankful I could be there with her and my sister and her family to hold her hand and touch her face. Together we created a sacred space of unconditional love and honor to embrace her and ease her spirit. She will long be remembered as a woman of beauty, wit, warmth, grace, and intelligence. Integrity was her highest value, and that's how she lived.

This is a call to me and an invitation to you:

- ⮞ to know our deepest values and live them fully;
- ⮞ to express our love now instead of waiting for the right time;
- ⮞ to tell the truth respectfully and listening with an open mind to the response;
- ⮞ to accept and celebrate that our own well-being is our responsibility;
- ⮞ to remember that the quality of our most important relationships is in our hands;
- ⮞ to live in both personal and profound integrity.

Having written this, I notice the part of me that felt shattered is gently mending with tender threads of gratitude and acceptance. The following is what I said at Mom's memorial service, June 30, 2007.

Rae Case Anderson

Born April 10, 1914, died May 11, 2007

Ah…to say good-bye to my mother. To never hear her sweet voice again; to never see her beautiful and animated face as she told me about her day, questioned me about mine; to never call her when I want guidance, support, or the best way to reach for something important to me; to never have her listen patiently to my stumbling words as I made me way toward clarity, compassionately listening, listening, and then she would say just the right thing to help me find my own way.

How very fortunate we are—my brother Roger, my sister Carolyn, our families, her grandchildren—to have Rae Case Anderson live ninety-three years and one month, years rich in love, laughter, and experiencing life to the fullest. My mom taught by example rather than lecture. What she believed was right, she did and encouraged in us. She demonstrated profound integrity.

Since her diagnosis of metastasized breast cancer in September, mom has talked more about her life story than any other time I can remember. In the last weeks at Carolyn's home, so many people—family, friends, and caregivers—sat and shared stories, laughter, tears, and such deep love and respect. Mom gave and received unconditionally and so very gracefully. What an honor to sit with her and review our lives together and apart.

My mom was a bit paradoxical, totally trusting her intellect and ability to do just about anything, except sing. She rode horses, was a Phi Beta Kappa, taught school, raised gloxinias, three amazing children, and corgis, loved my dad completely, danced with abandon, sailed, traveled the world, caught salmon, loved a good joke, was a great friend and cook, and oh my, she could remember the names of people in her life back to the beginning of time!

And then, curiously, she was self-doubting and shy when it came to her impact on others and her beauty. She was genuinely surprised, as well as gratified, when people remembered her as a positive force in their lives. And even at ninety-three she could never figure out why people thought she was beautiful.

Her beauty at the end was incandescent; she radiated such calm presence. She watched us with such intensity, drinking us in, every detail, and we were doing the same thing, letting her know with every touch, look, and word that we loved her.

I would like to share a poem with you by Mary Oliver that reveals my mom's passion for life.

When Death Comes

When death comes
like the hungry bear in autumn;
when death comes and takes all the bright coins from his purse

to buy me, and snaps the purse shut;
when death comes
like the measle-pox;

when death comes

like an iceberg between the shoulder blades,
I want to step through the door full of curiosity, wondering:
what is it going to be like, that cottage of darkness?

And therefore I look upon everything
as a brotherhood and a sisterhood,
and I look upon time as no more than an idea,
and I consider eternity as another possibility,

and I think of each life as a flower, as common
as a field daisy, and as singular,

and each name a comfortable music in the mouth,
tending, as all music does, toward silence,

and each body a lion of courage, and something
precious to the earth.

When it's over, I want to say: all my life
I was a bride married to amazement.
I was the bridegroom, taking the world into my arms.

When it's over, I don't want to wonder
if I have made of my life something particular, and real.
I don't want to find myself sighing and frightened,
or full of argument.

I don't want to end up simply having visited this world.

Dignity, honor, grace, humor, and a helping hand…we are saying good-bye to Rae in physical form. She lives on in us. We are her inspired legacy.

Thank you, Mom, for sharing yourself so completely with me…with us.

Reflections

1. After reading my definitions of integrity, take a moment and write your own definition.

2. Where in your life is your integrity solid, where you wouldn't even think about breaking your word or not keeping an agreement?

3. In what parts of your life do you have broken agreements and you haven't kept your word? What is the impact?

4. Think of someone in your life whose integrity is profound. What do you think they would tell you to do to rebuild your integrity? Will you do it?

Anni with me in Nepal

Let Your Light Shine

Is this a call to arms?
Not unless it is for arms to encircle
someone in need of tenderness.
Is this a call to arms?
Not unless it is for arms to point out a
new direction of peace and healing.
Is this a call to arms?
Not unless it is for arms to be a safety
net for those who are falling.
Is this a call to arms?
Not unless it is for our arms to entwine
courageously to take a stand for truth.
Is this a call to arms?
                    YES!

—Kris King

52

Let Your Light Shine
Even a Headlamp Can Be a Source of Inspiration

December 2007

Walking in the early morning is one of my favorite ways to greet my day, my world. In the stillness of early morning I get to witness the transition from darkness to light, the moon taking its final bow, stars seemingly dimming as the sun's rays touch the earth, deer gazing at me as I pass, and all the while feeling fresh air touch my body inside and out. Bliss.

The deep darkness of winter mornings was a challenge until I remembered my trusty headlamp that I use in camp in the evenings in Bhutan. When I realized I could use it on my morning walks at home, I shook my head, thinking, "What took you so long to figure out you could use your headlamp at home?" Well, I had my headlamp only associated with trekking in Bhutan, not walking in the dark at home.

This morning, as I was walking through a cool, dark mist, I kept looking at the light my head-lamp cast, always eight feet out ahead of me. Using that soft glow, I safely found my way even though the rest of my surroundings were still dark. And then tears sprang into my eyes as I felt a deep connection to my spirit, to everything. It was as if I had connected the dots between two points that I didn't know were disconnected. When I take ownership of my own light, I can see what I want ahead of me. The more ownership I take, the farther I can see.

This inspiration led to another. A favorite quote by Johann Wolfgang Von Goethe came to mind.

> I have come to the frightening conclusion that I am the decisive element. It is my personal approach that creates the climate. It is my daily mood that makes the weather. I possess tremendous power to make life miserable or joyous. I can be a tool of torture or an instrument of inspiration. I can humiliate or humor, hurt or heal. In all situations, it is my response that decides whether a crisis is escalated or de-escalated, and a person humanized or de-humanized. If we treat people as they are, we make them worse. If we treat people as they ought to be, we help them become what they are capable of becoming.

The morning has brightened enough that there is no need for my headlamp any longer. I take it off and look at it with gratitude. Yes, it is something I own and use; it is a great tool. The light I possess, my inherent gifts, talents, wisdom, love, humor, and intuition are all for me to use in this life the best way I know how to light my own way and to help light the way for others. The same is true for each of us.

You might have seen this before. Connect the dots using four straight lines without picking up your pen.

After some play you will discover that the only way to connect the dots is to draw outside the lines.

I believe that when you and I take full ownership of our light, it's easier to draw outside the lines of conventional thinking, limitations, and fears, to be creative, see the possibilities in each moment, and then to courageously use ourselves to make this the world we want to live in every day.

Let your light shine! And let me know of your adventures.

Reflections

1. What are things you do to take care of yourself physically that also support you spiritually?

2. What does, "It is my personal approach that creates the climate. It is my daily mood that makes the weather," mean to you?

3. After reading this book, what does this mean to you? "The light you possess, your inherent gifts, talents, wisdom, love, humor, and intuition are all for you to use in this life the best way you know how, to light your own way and to help light the way for others."

Kris King, 2008 *Photo by Christopher Briscoe*

Acknowledgments

So many people to acknowledge in a life as long and full as mine. And there are those who stand in the forefront. My eternal thanks to each of you.

My parents, my sister Carolyn, and brother Roger.

My husband, Kyle, and my sons, Matthew, Mark, and Kyle.

My surgeons, Dr. Murdock and Dr. Cutler.

My oncologist, Dr. Fitzgibbons.

My first great teacher of transformational education, Gary Koyen.

My first business partner, James Newton.

My friends and mentors, Linda Williamson and Bev Foster.

My friend, Sherrie Frank, who got this book rolling.

My committed and talented staff over the years.

The great people at Bridgeway Books who helped me fulfill a dream.

And every single person who has walked through the doors of Wings Seminars, trusted the process, and changed their lives the way they wanted to.

I am grateful and honored to share my life with you. Thank you!